Preach the Word of God

PREACH THE WORD OF GOD

by

FREDERICK M. MORRIS

Dean of the Cathedral Church of St. Mark,
Minneapolis

Foreword by

ALDEN DREW KELLEY

President and Dean of Seabury-Western
Theological Seminary, Evanston

MOREHOUSE-GORHAM CO.
NEW YORK
1954

PRINTED IN THE UNITED STATES OF AMERICA
BY THE HADDON CRAFTSMEN, INC., SCRANTON, PA.

To

CHARLES WARD SEABURY
whose interest and generosity make
possible the conduct of this annual
lectureship.

Foreword

THE ART of preaching is no easy one. But to write about it in any effective way is even more difficult. It is like talking about painting a picture, or lecturing on the composition of a sonata, or setting forth the technique of making love. It seems almost impossible to say anything specific without being dull, commonplace, and perhaps downright vulgar. And to talk in generalities is likely to be stilted and quite unhelpful.

The author of these lectures has notably avoided the usual pitfalls. Given as part of his course as Annual Lecturer in Preaching at Seabury-Western Theological Seminary, in Evanston, Illinois, the publication of these addresses will be welcomed by many who were not able to attend the series when and as delivered. Although the book is primarily directed to ministers and those studying for the ministry, there is included much of interest for the ordinary lay person.

It is the view of Dean Morris that preaching involves a dual and mutual responsibility. He recognizes and stresses the participatory role of the worshippers in the pews: "It takes a congregation to produce preaching quite as much as it does a speaker in the pulpit." Accordingly, the average church-goer will find much in the following pages which will merit his careful attention.

The author, who is now Dean of the Cathedral Church of St. Mark, in Minneapolis, writes from a varied experience as a preacher and as a teacher of preaching. The reader will agree, I think, that he has well explicated the bearing of the Gospel of God on human needs and aspirations and done it with sincerity and in a lively, thought-provoking style. We are grateful for the privilege of making more widely available this presentation by Dean Morris.

ALDEN DREW KELLEY

Preface

THIS BOOK is for laymen as well as clergy. Preaching is a subject about which laymen need instruction as much as clergy. Certainly there are many more laymen participating in the business of preaching than there are clergy. For hearers are as much participants as speakers.

The only chapters which are addressed solely to preachers are Chapters Seven and Eight. Even these, I hope, may have interest for the inveterate listeners as well as for the preachers themselves.

F. M. M.

Contents

The contents of this book were initially given as part of the Charles Ward Seabury Lectureship in Preaching for 1953-54, at Seabury-Western Theological Seminary, Evanston, Illinois.

Preach the Word of God

T AKE thou Authority to preach the Word of God.
—The Book of Common Prayer

G IVE GRACE, O heavenly Father, to all Bishops and other Ministers, that they may, both by their life and doctrine, set forth thy true and lively Word. . . . And to all thy People give thy heavenly grace . . . that, with meek heart and due reverence, they may hear, and receive thy holy Word.
—The Book of Common Prayer

1

Preach and Listen!

TO SAY that preaching is an exciting business
might sound incredible to some long-suffering
laymen and even to some preachers, oppressed
with the sense of drudgery and discipline. Yet exciting it is in its intended purpose and wonderfully often in its accomplished purpose. Until the
genuine recognition of that quality be a part of the
understanding of both preacher and hearer, the
value and effectiveness of preaching remains un-
fulfilled. Certainly the traditional Christian belief
as to the nature of preaching is exciting. And its
irrepressible persistence and vitality through the
ages make it an exciting historic phenomenon,
all the more so in the light of the very reasons
which, at first blush, might make incredulous these
same long-suffering laymen and drudgery-con-
scious preachers.

The overwhelming verdict of Christian history
has been that preaching is a divinely intended as-

pect of God's redemptive activity in human society. And the genuine acknowledgment of that
verdict is bound to awaken in the Christian believer an awareness of the fundamental element of
excitement in the nature and purpose of preaching.
To attempt to stimulate that awareness is the purpose of this book, in the fervent hope that thereby
the great privilege of preaching and hearing the
life-giving Gospel of Christ may be seen anew in
its true light.

No man should be presented for ordination to
the ministry who has not sensed and been moved
by that understanding of preaching. And surely
every one of us preachers already in the harness
welcomes the opportunity to be reminded and re-
awakened at regular intervals to the realization
of it all, so that we may "rekindle the gift of God
that is within" us through the laying on of hands
at Ordination. Furthermore, every layman can
profit greatly in being reminded to recognize and
contemplate the exciting potential in the nature
and purpose of preaching, so that he can regard
anew these admonitions of our Lord: "Take heed
how ye hear"; "He that hath ears to hear let him
hear."

The Christian Faith originated, grew, and

swept across the world to the echo of impassioned preaching. John the Baptist came preaching in preparation for the coming of the Lord. And there went out to hear him all the people of Judea and of Jerusalem. And from the moment of John's imprisonment, Jesus began to preach; wherever He went He preached, and great throngs heard Him gladly. And He chose twelve that He might send them forth to preach. And through all the centuries since, His Gospel has been preached with indefatigable persistence and vehemence in spite of every sort of obstacle and every sort of reason for discouragement and defeat. And everywhere it has been listened to with a degree of eager receptiveness and hungry desire far exceeding what one would have a right to expect in the light of any purely human enterprise. Often with astonishing power and effectiveness, often with lameness and inadequacy, at times clearly and explicitly, at times badly and with distressing distortion, frequently with most unfortunate admixture of heresy, the Gospel has been preached and preached, with an effect in human society far stronger than the human shortcomings of preachers deserve and far beyond the capacity of the human voice alone. Yes, there is much indeed that is exciting about this strange business of preaching. And when it is well done, and with flaming conviction, the results are exciting far beyond any expectation.

Whenever the voice of preaching has been restrained or censored, it has burst forth again with renewed vigor, often in unexpected quarters and in unexpected ways. Its undiminished zeal and vitality is one of the humanly inexplicable phenomena of history. He who spake by the prophets will have His say! And He will use the human voice for His vehicle despite all its inadequacies and shortcomings. Like the householder who allowed the wheat and the tares to grow together, lest in removing the tares the wheat be also destroyed, so the Holy Spirit seems to allow the weeds and the grain in preaching to flourish indiscriminately, lest in silencing the prattle the music of the Gospel be also stilled.

Even the Church cannot constrain or restrict the preaching of the Gospel. The Holy Spirit bloweth where He listeth, and He will not be subject to man-made restrictions nor neglects. Though the Church is indeed His habitation, He is still greater than the Church. When the human element in the Church neglects or abuses the heavenly command to preach, the divine displeasure is aroused,

and the consequences are bound to be tragic. It is
for us in each generation to rededicate ourselves
with renewed zeal and conviction to the task and
privilege of preaching, so that the Church may
fulfill her divine commission in this age and be,
in the most effective sense possible, the channel of
the Holy Spirit, whose Word must be proclaimed.
For indeed He will have His say! Woe is us if
we preach not the Gospel!

The Holy Spirit will not be without preachers
nor will He be without listeners; He *will* be heard,
and if people will not listen in the churches, the
voice of the Gospel will seek them out in the by-
ways and hedges. Whenever the human element in
the Church neglects the hearing of the Gospel,
just as when it neglects the preaching of it, the
divine displeasure is aroused and the consequences
are bound to be tragic. It is quite as important that
the people be reminded of the compulsion to hear
as that the clergy be reminded of the compulsion
to preach.

If anyone, priest or layman, takes the attitude
that the only way to get people to listen is to have
sermons of such a quality as to make them want
to do so without urging, he runs head-on into the
conflicting facts that our Lord put great and fre-

quent emphasis upon the obligation to heed, and that He Himself was not listened to by hosts of people. And who could presume to undertake to preach more effectively or more persuasively than He? God's command to His Church regarding the Word is twofold: "Go ye therefore and preach!" and "Take heed how ye hear!"

The preacher is to preach on the subject of preaching. He is to preach on the subject of heeding as part of the same business. People need sermons on the technique of listening, "that, with meek heart and due reverence, they may hear, and receive [His] Holy Word" quite as much as the clergy need instruction on the technique of preaching, "that they may, both by their life and doctrine, set forth [His] true and lively Word."

No individual alone can ever preach. It takes a congregation to produce preaching quite as much as it does a speaker in the pulpit. If we define preaching carefully, we must add that preaching is truly preaching only when it is both spoken and listened to in mutual faith concerning its nature and purpose. When preacher and people alike share in the conviction that it is a divinely ordained channel for the mediating of God's Word, then it is preaching indeed.

Preaching might also be defined as a two-way communications system between God and His people in which the preacher is the medium of transmission: the Godward movement is the expectant receptiveness with which the people reach out to meet the offered message, as well as the self-offering of the preacher to God.

The subject matter of preaching must include teaching the people to understand and to exercise their responsibility in this co-operative enterprise. Without that recognition of the need for right listening and without that faith in God's intended part, preaching comes to be regarded all too readily as a kind of competitive performance whereby the professional competence of various clergymen can be measured and compared. Or else it comes to be regarded as a type of religious entertainment, whereby a bid is made for the attention and attendance of an audience which, in this television age, is increasingly aware of its growing opportunities for diversion in the whole area of professional entertainment; and that is bound, from the start, to stack the cards against the Church, except in the case of those few preachers whose ability and reputations become nationally known.

You shall preach often on the Parable of the Soils, in which our Lord made very plain and explicit the responsibility for right hearing. You shall reiterate and re-emphasize His warnings— "Take heed how ye hear," and "He that hath ears, let him hear." The parable assumes that there is nothing the matter with the seed, which is the Word of God, and that there is nothing the matter with the methods of the sower, who represents the divine self-revelation. The failure of the seed to produce fruit was due to the unreceptiveness of the poor soils, just as the success of the harvest was due to the receptiveness of the good soil. We shall avoid, of course, any implication that there is nothing the matter with us preachers, or any implication that the sower in the parable represents us. But we shall insist that God intends preacher and people alike to share in the responsibility for keeping the soil receptive.

Many an average person, when he gets in church, sits back in an attitude which says, inarticulately but nonetheless definitely, "Well, here I am, and the preacher better make it good if he expects me to come back again, because I have plenty of important duties and interests to keep me quite busy. I have no time for second-rate preachers nor for listening to anything that is impractical or too religious to be of use to me."

Teach your people to be concerned more with the content of preaching than with matters of delivery and technique. I have known of numerous cases where people have "raved" about how wonderful a preacher was, perhaps largely basing their opinion on the fact that "he didn't use any notes," or some other equally irrelevant reason. But when asked what he said, they were at a loss to recall a single idea. This is not always entirely due to a paucity of ideas in the preacher's head; it is also due to an entirely inadequate basis for evaluating and listening to preaching on the part of the people.

You cannot hope to have the preaching in your church what you want it to be and what it ought to be until you have shared with your people your convictions as to what preaching means and what it is for. And you can make it a part and an illustration of the whole wide subject of the necessity for human response to the divine initiative and for human appropriating of the divine self-giving. "He that hath ears to hear let him hear"; "Take heed how ye hear."

There are also many sermons to be preached on the subject of God's use of human and material vehicles for His purposes: in the ministry, in the

Sacraments, in the mission of the Church, in the offerings of the people—all closely related to faith in this ministry of the Word and all deeply rooted in the theology of the Incarnation.

From the pulpit, then, inform your people about these aspects of preaching. Proclaim the faith whereby you presume to be a preacher. Convey to them your knowledge of the exciting implications of preaching in its claim to be God's action among us. The more that knowledge and that faith are shared by preacher and people alike, the more effective an instrument of God becomes the preaching of His Gospel. And as you affirm and reaffirm to your people your own faith and insights, these will grow deeper and deeper in your own life as well as in theirs; so it always has been and always will be in the mystery of shared faith.

An understanding and conviction concerning the nature of preaching, such as we have been attempting to formulate and clarify, lays a very special responsibility and obligation upon the preacher regarding his own life and relationships. In the light of the high and holy nature of his calling, the preacher is bound to be "a man set apart." And so it should be, despite the understandable rebellion which arises in his heart when he thinks upon the distortions of that idea implicit in the attitudes of many laymen. Preaching, in the sense in which we have been considering it, does not begin and end with mounting and descending from the pulpit on Sunday mornings. The life of the preacher and his relationships with people all through the week are bound to be a part of the performance of his task. "Practice what you preach" is a maxim deeply imbedded in the consciousness of the people. In its strictest sense, of course, it is an impossible admonition. No clergyman, so very human as he is, can presume to be a perfect pattern of Christian living and Christian character; nonetheless, he is "a man set apart" in a definite sense. And despite the frequency of superficial comments by laymen to the effect that they want their rector to be "a regular guy" and "one of the boys," in their heart of hearts and in their best moments they want him to be "different," and believe they have the right to find him so.

It is only natural for a clergyman to want to be considered no different from others; it is only human to want to identify oneself as far as possible with his fellows in this earthly pilgrimage. There are deep, instinctive impulses involved under the general heading of gregariousness which make a man reluctant to be separated from, different from others. One shrinks from the frequent gibes, the conventional cartoons, and the popular clichés which make clergymen appear as second-grade morons or blue-nosed puritans or queer ducks. The saying that there are three sexes—men, women, and clergymen—is gall and wormwood to us, no matter how we may laugh it off.

We are all familiar with, and not undisturbed by, comments which imply that clergymen are not quite human. This idea finds expression most generally at summer conferences, where young people exclaim with delight when they have discovered certain clergymen to be "human after all," as the result of having played baseball or tennis with them and having seen them perform with commendable horseplay, and even with a degree of semi-professional artistry, on stunt night. It is a sweet sound when someone says, "You don't seem like a minister at all," for it indicates some dispelling of the cloud of misconception which hovers never very far away from the head of every clergyman.

There is, however, a danger in all this which has betrayed many a priest and undermined many a potentially good and effective ministry. It has

led men into the habit of wishy-washy, hail-fel-
low-well-met preaching which may get appreci-
ative laughs from the congregation and send them
forth wagging their heads and avowing that the
parson is certainly "quite a guy." But that is a
sorry substitute for the faithful dispensing of the
Word. The "good fellow" preacher will win
friends and influence people for himself, but he
will do far less than he ought, or could, to exalt
Jesus Christ.

It is good to avoid like the plague any degree
of professionalism and any degree of taking oneself too seriously. Good spirits and human-ness in
the best sense, and a properly tolerant understanding of, and sympathy with, all aspects of the life of
people generally, are of the essence. Nonetheless,
clergymen are set apart whether they like it or
not, and the people, by and large, know that in
their hearts and want it that way.

Preach, then, on the subject of the special calling, the special responsibilities, the special burdens,
the special task of the ministry. Preach on the
necessity for clear thinking and deep believing
about all of this on the part of the laity. Preach on
the necessity for lay encouragement of the clergy
to be clergy in the best and highest sense, lest they

unwittingly contribute to the lowering of the standards of the ministry.

We shall refer later to the necessity for self-identification of preacher with people in a right sense. But for now we are to recognize the inevitable differences which must be. Any man who is afraid or reluctant to be set apart ought not to go into the ministry, for his understanding of its peculiar burdens and responsibilities is bound to be inadequate. Any man who has not a high and holy regard for the office of preacher or who shrinks from its demands and disciplines ought not to go into the ministry, for he is at odds with the doctrine and practice of the Church from the beginning. Any man whose convictions on this score do not so fill his heart and mind as to spill over into the awareness and beliefs of his people, so that they become sharers in the task of preaching, is doomed to frustration and ineffectiveness from the start.

Now no man can be a good preacher from the first moment, nor does the listener come naturally by a capacity to hear the Gospel with entire receptiveness and perception; both arts must be learned and cultivated. God can make you a good preacher if you offer to Him a high regard for your task and a disciplined eagerness to be taught. God can make of your people good listeners if they, by your help, bring to Him a lively faith and a humble desire to grow in the knowledge of the Lord.

Paul, an apostle of Christ Jesus by the will of God according to the promise of the life which is in Christ Jesus, to Timothy, my beloved child: Grace, mercy, and peace from God the Father and Christ Jesus our Lord.

I remind you to rekindle the gift of God that is within you through the laying on of my hands; for God did not give us a spirit of timidity but a spirit of power and love and self-control. Do not be ashamed then of testifying to our Lord, nor of me his prisoner, but take your share of suffering for the gospel in the power of God, who saved us and called us with a holy calling, not in virtue of our works but in virtue of his own purpose and the grace which he gave us in Christ Jesus. ... For this gospel I was appointed a preacher. ... Follow the pattern of the sound words which you have heard from me, in the faith and love which are in Christ Jesus; guard the truth that has been entrusted to you by the Holy Spirit who dwells within us.

2

"We Preach Not Ourselves"

IF PREACHING be a divinely ordained function of the ministry which is part of God's redemptive activity in His Church, it cannot be approached by any conscientious preacher without frequent qualms and misgivings. The higher one's valuation of, and conviction about, preaching, the greater will be his feeling of presumption in undertaking it. Human pride, however, is an insidious thing, and has a way of breaking through the wall at the very point where it is supposed to be least vulnerable. And so the greatest opportunities for humility often become the area where pride asserts itself most obtrusively.

Dr. John Oman has written in his book *Concerning the Ministry*, "Unless the pulpit is the place where you are humblest in giving God's message, it is certain to be the place where you are vainest in giving your own." That statement suggests the struggle which is bound to occur and re-occur in the spiritual life of a preacher.

In the next chapter we shall consider the problem of the preacher's misgivings and his need for encouragement and reassurance. But in this one we shall turn our attention to the problem of vanity, which is one of the most dangerous problems of all.

I love the story—undoubtedly familiar to you, but worth repeating and worth frequent recalling —of the ecstatic parishioner who said to the rector, after church, "That was a wonderful sermon!" To which the rector replied, "So the Devil whispered to me as I left the pulpit!" Unfortunately, not all preachers recognize the voice of the Devil when they hear it. Nor is it as unattractive a voice as one might wish.

And in this connection I am also reminded of the last meeting of my homiletics class, just before graduation, at the Virginia Seminary. Dr. Berryman Green, our distinguished teacher, said to us, "Gentlemen, you are about to go forth to many parts of the world and into many different kinds of situations. Yet wherever you go, there are bound to be young women who, after service, will take your hand in both of theirs and, looking you in the eye, will say, 'That was a wonderful sermon!' Gentlemen, the trouble is that some of you will believe it."

Not to believe it is a struggle. For too often our people seem to be on the side of the Devil in a conspiracy to sell the preacher down the river of vanity. Here is a desperate need for sermons on the subject of preaching. We can certainly tell our people first of all that proper church manners do not include the necessity for saying, after service, "I certainly enjoyed your sermon!" or "That was a wonderful sermon!" I am sure that many people regard such remarks as much *de rigeur* as telling your hostess when leaving a party that you have had a wonderful time.

The real question is not whether the sermon *is* wonderful or is *not* wonderful. It may very likely have been wonderful. In fact, there is an inescapable aspect of wonder about any sermon which touches and moves the heart with God's grace. The real question is the "wonderfulness" of the preacher, and the real difficulty and danger is taking unto oneself the glory that belongs to God. The real tragedy is personal vanity, for once it gets out of hand, it blocks God out, and the preaching actually does become a personal performance, no longer accomplishing anything save the diversion of the people. It has been said that if anyone tells you what a wonderful sermon you preached, you are to go home very soberly and tell God you are sorry. For a wonderful sermon will in truth send your people home to ponder upon it without discussing its merits with you.

Sermons are not ends in themselves. They are not exhibits to be held up for evaluation by curious and analytical spectators. Nor are they feats of oratorical prowess whereby the preacher makes evident to his people (and to visiting committees from other parishes looking for a rector) his own right to be admired and complimented (and called to "larger opportunities"). We clergy, being so very human, are already far too easy a prey for egocentricity and ambition to permit the laity to go uninstructed or unrebuked in this kind of evaluation of sermons. And we do well to include ourselves in any such rebuke.

I believe the advertising of sermon subjects in the papers and on bulletin boards outside the church to be singularly unfortunate. It encourages people to suppose that an attempt is being made to beguile them into going to church because the sermon subject is so intriguing. This leads very quickly to the idea that preaching and churchgoing itself are just another form of diversion competing for people's patronage. It also encourages the idea that all responsibility for a hearing rests upon the eloquence and persuasiveness of the preacher, together with his skill as a promoter, and leaves no sense of personal obligation on the part of people to seek out opportunities to hear or to give an offering of expectant receptiveness. Furthermore, I cannot believe it possible that anyone really goes into a church because the bulletin board outside is so utterly irresistible. Someone may do so occasionally, but the results in that respect could not possibly counteract the damage done in general.

Ours must be a constant struggle to avoid, as we would the plague, any prima donna attitude toward preaching, and we need the co-operation of our people in the battle. Our sermons are never to be evaluated on the false basis of the approval and applause of our listeners. To be content with winning a personal following of admirers and with building a congregation on the basis of friendship and loyalty to oneself is a never-ceasing temptation to the clergy and one in which the laity are all too ready to acquiesce. Applause and admiration are a heady brew, and it requires genuine humility and a clear understanding of the real purpose of the ministry, daily renewed, to avoid becoming confirmed addicts of that brew.

Our system of preferment subjects the clergy to terrific temptations. Every clergyman is tempted to envision himself as "a big man in the Church," besieged with calls to more-important positions. And he must struggle with the temptation to view his eloquence and skill in the pulpit as a means toward that end.

Tell the people what it is you are attempting to do in your preaching. Tell them that sermons are not meant to be enjoyed. Tell them that sermons are meant to accuse, to move, to enlighten, to stir, to inform, to reassure, and to save. Tell them that preaching is—to use an old saw—"to comfort the afflicted and afflict the comfortable." Tell them that preaching is meant to inform the ignorant, to challenge the erroneous, to take up arms against the heretic, to denounce the moral compromiser, to irritate the parsimonious, to give new vision to the faithful, to inspire the receptive, to restore the penitent, to encourage the despondent— but never just to entertain or divert. Above all, it is not meant to win admiration and applause.

Our Lord said, "Woe unto you when all men

speak well of you." And I believe that is peculiarly applicable to preachers. No man can preach the Gospel fully and conscientiously and at the same time avoid criticism and disapproval. If you never irritate any of your people you may be sure you are not doing your job well. If nobody ever transfers out of your parish because they cannot stand your preaching, then you should beware. The undermining of pet clichés, the repudiation of popular heresies, and the pricking of consciences are going to fret and annoy people. Some will reject the opportunity offered for new insights or new understandings in such preachments and instead will speak ill of you. This will not only wound your pride and hurt your feelings but will also make you uneasy about the rightness of your stand or your policy.

Vanity demands that a clergyman please everybody, not only in the pulpit but in all his doings. To proceed as though that were desirable, or even possible, is bound to lead not only to betrayal of one's primary responsibilities and obligations but also to grave unhappiness and misery. I shall never forget the remarks made to me along this line many years ago by a wise vestryman. I was young and eager to please my congregation and to have nothing but happy relations with everybody.

When differences arose as to policies of administration, and exceptions were taken and expressed as to convictions spoken in the pulpit and even to the subjects chosen upon which to preach, I was very unhappy and disturbed. I felt it was incumbent upon me to justify everything I did and to argue all opponents into agreement. My unhappiness must have been very evident, for this vestryman spoke up one time and said, "Young man, if you think you can please everybody, then you're attempting to do what even our Lord Himself could not do." I became aware of my presumption and my vanity in the light of his rebuke, and the experience has never ceased to be helpful and reassuring to me.

The problem of vanity cannot be left there, however. For vanity not only prompts us to seek popularity and applause at any cost, but also to be arrogant. Now arrogance cares not whether people are pleased or not. It vaunteth itself, is puffed up, behaves itself unseemingly, and seeketh its own. It expresses itself in pride of office. It says, "Because I am a clergyman I can do no wrong. Because I am a clergyman you must do as I say without question. If we differ, you may be sure that you are wrong—because I am right!"

This kind of attitude makes itself evident in the

pulpit very readily. I believe there is little choice in degree of evil between the preacher who is soft and flabby and superficial because he is trying to please everyone and make himself popular, and the preacher who is arrogantly sure of himself and uses the pulpit as though it were a papal throne from which to hurl his bulls and edicts. I know of only one cure or preventative for that type of pride, and that consists of the regular reading of, and meditating upon, the following passage from Holy Writ:

> Ye know that the princes of the Gentiles exercise dominion over them, and they that are great exercise authority upon them. But it shall not be so among you: but whosoever will be great among you, let him be your minister; And whosoever will be chief among you, let him be your servant: Even as the Son of man came not to be ministered unto, but to minister and to give his life a ransom for many (K.J.V.).

Somewhere between apologetic softness and arrogant hardness one's course must be steered.

Of course, the note of "this means you" must never be missing from sermons, because one of the hardest things for us poor mortals to encompass is the personalizing of moral truth. "I wish my husband had been present to hear that sermon," or "That sermon was just what these people need," are compliments of a very dubious sort, for they are evidence of the everlasting tendency in all of us to apply to everyone else except ourselves the probings of the Holy Spirit. That which we acknowledge to be good and necessary for humanity as a whole, we often consider not applicable to ourselves, because we consider ourselves wiser or more responsible or more perceptive than the average run of people. We decry the sins and passions of others which make the world so dark, yet our own sins and passions we blame upon the bad social environment of our youth or upon the neuroses of our parents, and belittle the tragic consequences of them. We bewail the breakdown of the Christian ideal of marriage in our society and feel critical toward the guilty persons, but we find little to be improved upon in our own marriages. We are very vocal in our condemnation of corruption and greed in government and in business generally, but we regard lightly our own individual greed and moral compromises, calling them by such euphemisms as "irresponsibilities." We are deeply disturbed and frightened by the warmongers who keep the world in turmoil, but we are bothered little by the trampling angers and ambitions and animosities in our own personal lives. Yes, we could go on indefinitely pointing out examples of this deep-rooted reluctance within the human breast to personalize moral truth.

Much preaching must be directed toward this objective of bringing people to ask, "Lord, is it I?" when confronted by the finger of accusation; a wonderful text is that question, "Lord, is it I?" In that scene of the Last Supper where our Lord said, "One of you shall betray me," we might well have supposed that the Apostles began at once to ask, "Lord, is it John?"—"Is it Peter?"—"Is it Andrew?" But they asked, "Lord, is it I?"

The Parable of the Last Judgment is another homiletical gem toward that end. The sheep and the goats alike asked, in effect, "Who, me?" both when they were commended and when they were accused. While it was easy for them to understand how other people were involved in these things, it came as a surprise that they themselves were involved, even though unwittingly. The story of David and Nathan, the lesson for the first Sunday in Lent, is another magnificent illustration of how a man can become shocked and indignant about what he was led to suppose was the injustice of someone else, when all the time it was his own sin which was being described.

Yes, preaching must sound strongly and courageously the note "This means you!" even if it must be at the cost of resentment toward the preacher on the part of those who are made uncomfortable. And not only must the note be struck that "this means you" but also the note that "this means me." Much good and true content in preaching has been vitiated by the preacher's apparent assumption of the role of judge and paragon. He may not mean to, he may not intend to, but it is an easy trap in which to fall. Perhaps that is why one dictionary definition of the word *preach* is "to converse in didactic monologue," and why in common usage it conveys the idea of sitting in judgment upon others in a censorious, unsympathetic manner.

Of course preaching must *include* censure and reproach. It must accuse and admonish. It must reprimand and denounce. Without these things it is too innocuous and too insipid to deserve to be called Christian preaching. But the preacher must let his people know that he and they are in it together. He must let them know for sure that his knowledge of sin and weakness has been learned quite as much from firsthand experience with himself as from experience with others. Equally requisite with sounding the note of "this means me" in that kind of preaching is some evidence of firsthand religious experience. When one preaches on the blessings and glory of the personal experiencing of Christ, it is obvious to a listener with any discernment at all whether it is out of a book or out of life. When one preaches on faith, the depth of one's own conviction, as distinguished from theoretical acquiescence, is all to easily detectable by the people. Genuine humility and evidence of real personal experience bring to preaching a dimension which gives depth and life and power to counteract and make unimportant the elocutionary shortcomings of the preacher. When a preacher keeps constantly in mind the fact that his people want to know what these things mean to him personally, he will avoid unreality in his preaching and will find easier the avoidance of the dangers of professional vanity.

The battle with "I" is at once the most bitter and the most important struggle of all human living. It is something with which all people are intimately familiar. It is something in which our people look to us for help and understanding and leadership. They do not expect us to be perfect; in fact, they prefer that we not be perfect. But they have a right to see evidence in us of a genuine courage and zeal in the battle, even though there may be frequent defeats. If they see that, they know they have not only a leader but a companion, and they will heed his voice and give thanks to God that they have such a pastor and such a preacher of the Word.

In the first chapter we considered at some length the importance and significance of receptiveness as the offering which the laity must contribute to preaching. The preacher must also be a recipient as well as a giver. And being a recipient is not easy for any human being, whether priest or layman.

From the human point of view, the position of donor is always preferable to that of recipient. Being a donor supports the ego; being a recipient requires admission of need and dependence. It is much easier and more attractive to human nature, apart from the grace of God, to enjoy the feeling of superiority and the condescension and the self-importance of giving or bestowing. It puts others in our debt and makes them beholden to us. It emphasizes the possessions or endowments or position that we have, as contrasted with the needs of those to whom we give. We don't like to receive because to do so is a kind of admission of inferiority or deficiency on our part. We don't like to be dependent upon, or beholden to, anyone. To be a receiver, genuinely and gratefully, requires a special strength of character and clarity of perception which, in turn, need the help of God for their development.

All this is to be proclaimed by the preacher to his people. And even as he does so, he must never forget that it also applies to himself, for he is in a peculiarly difficult position. His very task aggravates the human tendency to be a giver rather than a recipient. He must remind himself constantly that he cannot give except he first receive. He can never forget that he is called to give only what he receives. Just so far as he allows himself to think and proceed on the premise that he is giving of his own inherent store of wisdom, so far does he vitiate the effectiveness of his preaching. We preach not ourselves, but Christ. As we move more firmly and more humbly in that conviction and by that confidence, so do we receive more richly and therefore preach more truly.

3

"Be of Good Cheer"

AS WE recognized in the beginning of the preceding chapter, any consideration of the holy
significance of preaching as a divine imperative,
and of the grave danger of the preacher himself
getting in the way of God who seeks to use him as
a channel, is bound to fill the heart of a conscientious priest with serious misgivings and to make
requisite and necessary some very real encouragement and reassurance.

To the theological student particularly, and to
a considerable extent to every parson, the problem
of "getting up a sermon" for every one of the Sundays that stretch ahead endlessly into the future,
with only six short days between each one, is apt
to loom rather too large. In fact it can loom so
large as to make the necessity for godliness and
humility seem a comparatively insignificant matter.

Certainly I can remember the impulse, as a

theological student, to exclaim, "How in the world can I be much concerned about vanity and ego-centricity in the pulpit, when I am so over-whelmed with doubt as to being able to get into the pulpit at all, prepared to say something, every blessed Sunday through all the years that lie ahead?" Even after having found by the experi-ence of over twenty years that that problem has somehow or other been encompassed—God only knows how—I still have times of dismay and doubt as to whether or not I can continue to make the grade in this respect.

However, that is in reality a secondary problem and one in which the Lord will indeed be with us if we allow Him. It is for us to affirm our faith in His power and will to use us, and to be deter-mined that we shall speak for Him rather than for ourselves:

> And Jesus [said] to them. . . . the gospel must first be preached to all nations. And when they bring you to trial and deliver you up, do not be anxious beforehand what you are to say; but say whatever is given you in that hour, for it is not you who speak, but the Holy Spirit.

The situations into which He knew His Apos-tles would be thrust, and concerning which He spoke these words, were not comparable to the un-opposed mounting of the pulpit week by week in an "eminently respectable" Episcopal church. But surely the principle and the faith are the same, and those words have been greatly reassuring and comforting to me through the years. "Do not be anxious beforehand what you are to say; but say whatever is given you in that hour, for it is not you who speak, but the Holy Spirit."

This chapter is intended to be one of encouragement and reassurance in the face of the many misgivings and feelings of inadequacy which assail us all. And the first thing that needs to be said is this: in your times of deepest misgiving and when your sense of inadequacy is greatest, you will be most effective in your preaching. The only thing to worry about with any justification is the failure to be assailed often enough and deeply enough with the sense of misgiving and inadequacy.

No one has preached for very long without making the discovery that the sermons preached from the greatest depths of preliminary dissatisfaction and misgiving are, amazingly often, the ones most effective in touching the hearts of the people. Perhaps it is partly because we labor harder in preparation over those which do not seem so good in anticipation. But I believe it is more largely because under these circumstances, we enter the pulpit more humbly conscious of our need for God's help.

If a man is sufficiently uneasy and sufficiently conscious of his inadequacy and sufficiently convinced of the holiness of his responsibility, he is going to be driven by the pressure of these factors to work hard. No one can take casually that which truly moves him to a sense of need. The natural inertia and distaste for discipline, which flourish in the make-up of us all, have no antidote so effective as a humble sense of personal inadequacy before a great and holy task to which one is committed.

It should be said that when our Lord told His Apostles not to be "anxious beforehand," He was not encouraging laziness or indifference. To be anxious is to be worried and fretted and without proper faith; to be deeply concerned and humbly determined is quite another matter. To approach preaching without anxiety is entirely different from approaching it without adequate, conscientious preparation. By our holy regard for our task we are to be spurred to genuine, painstaking, hard work. Nothing can be substituted for hard work, and hard work will bear fruit. For God makes wonderful use of hard work, and this is cause for very real and heartfelt encouragement.

When a man gives to the task of preaching an honest degree of disciplined, sustained work, together with faith in God's will to use him, though he lack any special gift of eloquence, though he possess no rare brilliance and no unusual native talents, he shall indeed be a faithful dispenser of the Word of God. And that is certainly cause for reassurance and encouragement, because anyone can work hard if he makes up his mind to it.

Nothing can take the place of hard work. The substitution of "the gift of gab," no matter how great the gift, is to throw an obstacle in the way of the Holy Spirit. I cannot believe that any real fruit will be borne under such conditions, no matter how carried away with delight the preacher may be in the awareness of his gift, nor how captivated his congregation may be in seeing and hearing him exercise it. To rely upon the gift of gab instead of upon hard work in preaching is to grieve the Holy Spirit and to blaspheme one's calling. The fact that it pleases people can prove to be a sorry substitute indeed for the light and grace of God which the gabbiness of the preacher is cutting off from his people. It must be readily admitted that the gift of gab can carry a man to high places of ecclesiastical preferment; it is a very effective weapon to wield on one's way to the top. But many a soul is lost on the way, both among the unfed sheep by the roadside and among the successful climbers en route to their destiny. For every one with the gift of gab who gets away with it, there are ten who think they are getting away with it and don't. It is indeed a dangerous thing on which to depend.

The story is told of a preacher who stood in the pulpit one Sunday and announced to his congregation that he had not found time in the preceding week to prepare a sermon. Hence, he was putting himself entirely in the hands of the Holy Spirit for the next twenty minutes. After the service, one of his wardens approached him and said— one can only hope with subtle irony—"Young man, I congratulate you. When you do your own work, you are better than God!"

Nothing can take the place of hard work. For the beginner in preaching there is to be found confidence and reassurance in the fact that genuine hard work and self-discipline will be implemented increasingly and effectively by the Holy Spirit, despite the lack of singular gifts and capacities to start with. As for us preachers already in harness, it is never superfluous to be reminded that there is probably room for improvement in the best of us and that taking a new lease on hard work and self-discipline offers new encouragement and new inspiration as we face the Sundays yet to come. Hard work is the surest means possible for putting into the hands of the Holy Spirit material which He will delight to use in conveying the power and the glory of the Gospel to the hearts and minds of His faithful people. (At a later time in our thinking together we shall go further into the matter of work, examining the way in which to go about it, and for what immediate purposes we should expend our efforts.)

Another encouraging fact to remember is the relationship between preaching and faithful pastoral work. The hard-working, self-sacrificing pastor, though a poor preacher by conventional standards, will find that his people listen gladly and to their eternal spiritual benefit because of what he means to them as a friend and shepherd. Here is one of the most vivid evidences of the mystic dimension in preaching. Love and zealous faith and consecration speak their own overtones in the words which come from the lips of the preacher. On the other hand it must be said, trite though it be, that lack of love and zealous faith and consecration can nullify to a tragic degree the most articulate and eloquent preaching imaginable. It is everlastingly true that what a man is can speak so loudly that it will drown out the sound of what he says.

Just as it is true that nothing can take the place of hard work in the immediate task of preparing to preach, so it is true that nothing can take the place of faithful pastoral labors, in season and out. The doorbell-ringing rector not only makes a churchgoing people but a gladly receptive and attentive people.

The story of Pentecost surely teaches us that there is a universal language of the soul which can transcend not only differences in tongues but also inadequacies in eloquence or lack of great skill in the use of words; and from all this we can take new courage and new confidence, for everyone of us can work hard and faithfully at being pastors. The old saying that religion is caught as well as taught is worth remembering.

The constant pastoral contact with your people is a most fruitful source of sermon material. The situations that are met, the questions that are asked, the hungers that are revealed, the needs that become evident, and the misconceptions that make themselves plain in the round of pastoral calling give rise to preaching that is alive and relevant to human needs, preaching that can be worthy of your divine commission.

There is another basis for reassurance: the recognizing and remembering that the Christian Gospel has an inherent power and truth of its own. It has its own compelling attraction, its own irresistible beauty, its own saving grace. It speaks to hungers and responses that are inherent in human make-up. It is not a message basically alien to life. The preacher does not have to bridge a chasm between two mutually irreconcilable realities of God and man—the very Gospel we have to preach is the reconciliation of the two in Christ. The chasm between man's self-will and the purpose of God has been bridged by Christ, and the message of that bridging is one which man wants to hear more than anything else that could be imagined. Preaching the Gospel is not a matter of attempting to make interesting and significant what is essentially dull and irrelevant; the Christian Gospel is incredibly exciting and thrilling.

Nothing under the sun could be more fascinating, more astounding, more breathtaking than the subject matter of the Gospel. One can say that it is sheer fantasy, that it is all rubbish, that it is a figment of the imaginations of self-deluded optimists. But for anyone to say that it is dull or uninteresting or unexciting is to prove that he hasn't the faintest idea of what it really means. If there is any apathy or boredom on the part of the hearers of sermons, it is not so much due to lack of charm and eloquence on the part of the preacher as it is to his failure to proclaim the authentic Christian Message.

The prevention or cure for such apathy and boredom will be found in consecrated determination to make one's preaching a constant declaration of the central message. The preacher must, of course, first see and experience for himself the exciting incredibility and the thrilling implications of the Gospel. Then his own excitement in belief will, by the power of the Spirit, be conveyed contagiously to the hearts and minds of his listeners in the affirming of the facts of this astonishing message.

There is indeed reassurance and encouragement to be found in the remembering of these facts about the inherent quality of the Gospel. It relieves the preacher of the necessity for creating the attractiveness and power of his message by means of his own skill and craftsmanship or by means of his own personality and charm. (Most of us quite accurately suspect that our skill and personal charm leave much to be desired.) Furthermore, those who do have the requisite skill and charm are treading on dangerous ground if they get into the way of substituting those gifts for the content of the Gospel message.

Finally, there is reassurance and encouragement in recognizing and remembering that the Gospel is definite and positive. The preacher's task lies not in thinking up something to say; it has already been said. His is not the responsibility for unearthing the treasure; it has already been revealed. His task is to proclaim, to declare, to affirm, and to emphasize this story of what God has done for His people through the ages and is doing for them through eternity. And this story of His mighty doings is told in a thousand ways throughout the Holy Scriptures.

The preacher's task is not so much to explain as to declare. Most of what he has to say is beyond explanation. The chief burden of his declaration cannot be diagnosed or dissected in the mind. His job includes interpreting, clarifying, and illustrating the Gospel as far as possible in the idiom and thought-forms of our time and our culture. He is to clothe it, as much as possible, in terminology which commands recognition from the generation in which we live. It is to be applied to the conditions and circumstances peculiar to our present history. But in doing this the preacher must be zealously determined and meticulously careful that it is always the Christian Gospel he preaches and not some modernistic caricature or some small fragment of it.

The heart of the message is, of course, summarized in the Creed. And that affirmation contains all the elements necessary to prove the thrill and the wonder of what the Church exists to conserve and proclaim. That Almighty God came down from heaven in the form of man and entered into the everyday business of human living is a claim startling and incredible enough in itself. No wonder people argue and balk at the threshold of believing it. To insist that God in human form, whom we know as Jesus, is both God and man— really God and really man; not "just like" God but very God of very God; not just appearing like a man but actually "made man" within the limitations of the flesh, as we are—that is double-talk! It is astonishing that otherwise intelligent-appearing men can say they believe anything so fantastic!

But that's not all by any means. Not only did God come down from heaven to be made man, but He suffered and died at the hands of men. It gets more astonishing all the time. Dorothy Sayers has written in her little book *Creed or Chaos?* "That God should play the tyrant over man is the dismal story of unrelieved oppression; that man should play the tyrant over man is the usual dreary record of human futility; but that man should play the tyrant over God and find Him a better man than himself is an astonishing drama indeed."

But the story goes further than that! This God-man was buried in a tomb and three days later came back to life, and lived and talked with His friends for many days and finally disappeared from their sight, leaving them transformed so that, from then on, they behaved like men possessed and went out into the world accomplishing things that they themselves never supposed they could. And the story goes on and on. Ever since that time this God-man has been doing things to people and causing them to do things such as nothing else or no one else has ever remotely approached.

The message of the Creed also says that by His death He saved men from the power of sin to destroy, that He restored the broken relationship between God the Creator and His creature, man —the relationship which man's sin had broken. And by His rising from the dead He opened to men the gates of Heaven. Further, He left us a Church in which He would continue to dwell and where men could always come to find Him, the serving, building, and expanding of which would be the serving of God's will.

Yes, it is a definite, positive, revealed Gospel that we have to proclaim. And we can take courage and be assured in our utter dependence upon that for our effectiveness as preachers. Be of good cheer! Lift up your hearts! For the Lord will be with you, even unto the end of the world.

4

The Will to Believe

THE CHRISTIAN Religion makes the command to believe no less emphatic than the command to preach. Our task as preachers is not to make believers out of our people so much as to help and stimulate them into making believers out of themselves. We are to preach on the subject of believing. We are to preach on the subject of the will to believe. We are to preach on the meaning of faith, on the glory of faith, on the triumph of faith, on the mystery of faith. And we are to drive home the idea of one's own responsibility for his faith.

I recognize, of course, the dangers of oversimplifying the mystery of faith. I recognize that there are many ways of entrance into the world of faith. I am quite aware of the part God plays, and that the fullness of faith is, in the last analysis, divinely bestowed. I know that the light sometimes breaks with unexpected suddenness and that there is no fixed pattern according to which our faith is born and nurtured. But experience has convinced me that this one aspect of the part to be played by the will is too little-recognized by people. And so I say we must challenge our people to believe, to dare to believe, to launch out upon the adventure of belief: we must *proclaim the divine command* to believe.

We are not to try to invoke faith by explaining everything, because there is always much that will ever remain inexplicable. The attempt to explain everything is a common and dangerous pitfall for preachers. We are not to try to wheedle people into faith by rationalizing and simplifying everything, because there will always remain much beyond reason and much that is not simple. We shall not attempt to argue people into faith willy-nilly. There is no escaping the element of adventure and risk in faith. We are to preach for a verdict; we are to demand a decision. Rather than assume total responsibility for our people's faith, or the lack of it, we shall lay that responsibility upon them. To this end we will preach many times on the Parable of the Soils, in which our Lord Himself makes clear and inescapable this idea of one's own responsibility in believing as well as in hearing.

Tell the people that there is no such thing as a ready-made faith, no such thing as an unquestioning faith, no such thing as freedom from the pressure of doubt and misgiving. Tell them that no man has ever been made to believe against his will nor even without the actual support of his will—no, not even by the most watertight arguments in the world. Not even our Lord Himself could persuade people when they chose not to be persuaded. And He rejected the temptation to win them by means of spectacular demonstrations of His power, demonstrations which would by-pass the requirement of sober and deliberate choice. The preacher's task is to stimulate and encourage his people in the raising of their hearts and minds and wills to that act of self-commitment which is the first step into faith.

The Gospel, by its very nature, is bound always to remain beyond the power of the mind alone to dissect and digest. Condemned to failure in advance is any effort by the preacher to sweep his people into that mysterious realm of faith by the power of inescapable logic. He must resist at any cost the tendency to win people into what they think is faith by diluting the otherworldliness of the Gospel or by jettisoning its mystery or by oversimplifying its profundities. The preacher must attack with every tool at his disposal the idea, deeply-rooted in the minds of many moderns, that preaching is intended above all else to argue the case, to beat down misgivings, to explain away all difficulties, to make plausible the incomprehensible, to knock the pins out from under skepticism, to allay all doubts, and, finally, to make the road to faith so smooth and easy that one just coasts along it almost in spite of himself, until he suddenly and happily finds that he has ended up in a state of universal salvation.

It comes as a surprise to many people to be told that faith is something in which control by the will plays a significant part. They suppose that faith cannot be bidden to come or go. They suppose that belief or skepticism is just the inevitable result of proof or the lack of it. They suppose that believers are believers because all their doubts have been removed by listening to some able preacher or by reading the right books; they suppose that skeptics are skeptics because no one has been able to remove their doubts for them—more or less in the way that one would have his appendix removed.

It is very fashionable in our day for skeptics to regard believers as being a little naïve or a little less than completely honest. Skepticism is looked upon very generally as a sign of superior intelligence or superior integrity, whereas faith is regarded as a kind of gullibility or credulity into which the less well-informed and the less brilliant might be expected to fall.

What we need to stress in our preaching about faith is that we believe what we believe because we *choose* so to believe. And this is just as true of the materialist or the determinist or the atheist as it is of the Christian. To suppose that one's position is the result of inescapable logic, as do unbelievers—especially among the intelligentsia— is to be self-deluded in a most profound sense. We are Christians because we choose to be. We are Christians because, like the Centurion we cry, "Lord, I believe! Help thou mine unbelief." We are Christians because we *choose* Christ as our Lord and as the final Answer to life's meaning; we choose Him out of a welter of confusing possibilities among which one *must* choose.

One cannot prove by logic the truth of the Christian Revelation, but it is equally true that one cannot prove by logic the materialistic or the deterministic or any other conflicting answer to the problem of life's meanings and values. Life *forces* us to make a choice because we have to begin the business of living with no delay. We cannot substitute a blind logic for the inexorable responsibility of choice. We cannot have the easy relief of refuge in logic. Christian discipleship means betting one's life on Christ. It is choosing to go ahead as though the Christian Revelation were true. It is proceeding on the great *assumption* that this is the path of life. And assurance is found as the result, not as the precursor, of this choice and this commitment. Whatever ultimate assurance we find will be at the end of a forced march. No such assurance can ever come to a bystander or spectator though he remain at his point of observation to the end of eternity.

This must be made clear to our people in order that they may understand the reasonableness of the command to believe. Far too many of them suppose that faith is an unquestioning state of mind and spirit into which a comparatively few fortunate souls are able to enter. And they want to be free from the struggle with doubts and uncertainties. They suppose they *ought* to be free from it. And so they say, wistfully, "I wish I had an unquestioning faith like yours." To which we must reply, both from the pulpit and in personal counseling and with all the emphasis at our command, that such is not the case even with the saints. Faith is wrought by ever-renewed choices and ever-renewed self-commitments in the face of all manner of testings and trials and doubts and misgivings which are bound to assail all human flesh. That is why faith is both a victory and a virtue: "This is the victory that overcometh the world, even our faith" (K.J.V.). And faith is not anything so negative as the mere absence of misgivings or doubts; it is rather a positive, vital conquest of the corroding, paralyzing effects of skeptical, overcautious hanging-back.

A young woman once told me that she thought most preachers take the faith of their people too much for granted. She went on to observe that when she did go to church (and it is only fair to say that she didn't go very often), it seemed as though it were assumed that she believed many things which she knew she didn't believe, and she thought that more time and effort should be given to clarifying difficulties and answering questions and resolving doubts. She also revealed, unknowingly, that she had very little conception of what it means to have faith in the Christian sense.

(And I believe she had a better case against the preachers she had heard for not telling her what faith is than for not brushing away for her all the doubts and questions which assailed her.) When I told her that she could believe if she made up her mind to it and set her will to it, she was at first resentful and shocked at my "obscurantism." But when I had been allowed to further clarify the concept for her, she admitted to being able to glimpse a brand new idea of what faith is.

It must also be made clear and emphatic that faith is not gullibility or credulity. There are those—we generally call them fundamentalists— who regard and teach faith as though it *were* obscurantism. Perhaps that is one reason why the whole idea is so widely regarded with suspicion in our society, especially in educational circles and among those whom *Time* magazine calls the "eggheads."

A little boy in Church School, when asked to define faith, answered, "Faith is believing what you know isn't true." Unfortunately, such a conception of faith is not limited to little boys. Faith, in the Christian sense, is neither believing what one knows isn't true nor believing without full and free use of the mind. Faith without reason is sentimental inanity, just as reason without faith is spiritual myopia. When faith and the intellect meet in mutual respect, both are enhanced and glorified. The course of faith must always be steered between that open-mindedness which is really empty-headedness and that blind acceptance which is mental paralysis: intellectual contentiousness and intellectual complacency are equally abhorrent to the Christian idea of faith.

We must recognize clearly that our preaching is being done in an age that worships "reason" and is therefore an age of intellectual arrogance. Skepticism is fashionable. Doubt is *de rigueur*. Many of our institutions of higher learning are generally committed to the position that Christianity is a negligible factor both in history and in philosophy, and that idea has permeated our society to a well-nigh lethal degree. Ours is an age of disbelief in a very special sense. As Dr. McCrady of the University of the South has said, "Ours is one of those recurrent periods in history when men imagine they are too wise to believe in God." To ignore or to belittle in our preaching this state of mind and spirit would be a tragedy.

Two of the chief epithets directed against Christianity by the intelligentsia (when, indeed, they bother to have anything to say about it at all) are "credulous escapism" and "unscientificness." They say we find in our faith escape from the hard realities of a strictly material order by credulous acceptance of undemonstrable spiritual values. Incidentally, it is interesting to note how similar this is to the Communist claim that religion is an "opiate of the masses." They tell us that religion is a projection of our longing for comfort and security which is really a subconscious desire to return to our mother's womb, thereby to escape from a life that has no ultimate meaning. Of course, they do not consider it necessary to explain *why* anyone should care about ultimate meaning, anyway, or *why* anyone should want security and comfort other than food and shelter such as can be secured outside the womb.

But be that as it may, we Christians reject the accusation of escapism and say that it is the materialists who are escapists. They are only doing what Christianity says is natural for man to do, namely, to run away from God. For to confront God is the most terrifying and distasteful thing a man can anticipate, especially when God is nailed to a cross. And the easiest way to deal with that problem is to deny Him. Surely we need to preach many sermons on what it means to confront God, and on the tragedy of attempting to run away from Him.

As for our being credulous, we can only reply that such people permit themselves to believe the most incredible improbabilities of accident and coincidence behind the facts of this creation and of this strange species called man. And I say "permit themselves" to believe, because here, too, we find to be inescapable the element of choosing that which we believe. They permit themselves to believe what to us are unbelievable improbabilities of coincidence; we choose to believe in the Christian interpretation of life. And there is nothing uncongenial to us about admitting the inescapableness of willful choice, for it is part and parcel of the whole Christian concept of this virtue called faith.

To say that religion is unscientific may be quite true in a sense, but it is more relevant to say that science is unreligious; it all depends on what you start with as the basic standard of value. That something is unscientific means nothing to us unless the subject under consideration is, by its nature, measurable by scientific standards. Poetry is unscientific. Love is unscientific. Beauty is unscientific. And religion is unscientific. But neither poetry nor love nor beauty nor religion are to be discarded because of that. Whether or not a matter is scientific is not necessarily the ultimate criterion of its truth.

It is indeed most important that we be familiar, both intellectually and spiritually, with the temper of our times. It is of greatest importance that we preach faith in the light of that temper, and that our people be sure we are not living and thinking in a cloistered vacuum apart from the pressures and problems which beset them. It is also important to avoid being argumentative and contentious. Intellectual contentiousness and finickiness are characteristic of the modern-day climate, especially as it originates in our colleges and universities. But you certainly are not going to overcome contentiousness with more contentiousness. No converts can be won by arguments. The battle is not to be joined on the line of logical conflict, despite all the talk these days about ideologies. It is faith that men want. It is faith which alone can satisfy the immortal pangs which gnaw at the vitals of humanity.

You are to preach the meaning and nature of faith. You are to relate it clearly to the temper of the times, and make plain its affinity for sound reason and intellectual integrity. You are to preach the necessity for deliberate choice and self-commitment. You are to preach your own discovery of the glory and depth of assurance which God gives to those who have made the choice and have given their lives back to Him.

The depth and vitality of your own faith will in itself be a message that moves and persuades. The extent of your own commitment will make itself readily felt. The strength of your own convictions, contrary evidence notwithstanding, will be a source of courage and zeal to your people. To show forth as well as to preach the nature and power of faith is the holy task to which a preacher is called. When that is coupled with an evident integrity of intellect and a glad willingness to face and to ponder any interpretation of the truth which may come to one's attention, then faith appears unmistakably as the way of light and strength, and to it people will be drawn and attracted because they see for themselves what it can do for a man.

"Repent and believe!" This has always been, and will always remain, one of the basic and elementary proclamations of the Christian Revelation. It is the signpost at the beginning of the road called faith, and to it we preachers are called to point our people with insistent emphasis; it is life eternal to which the roadway leads.

5

"Preach Christ!"

IN THINKING together about the mystery of faith, we have already taken note of the fact that it cannot be confined within specified bounds. Nor can the means of entering the realm of faith be cut to any unalterable pattern. There must always remain the elements of mystery, and unpredictability, and "givenness." The will and the mind must both be brought into action. There is always the inescapable element of choice and decision and self-commitment in the adventure of believing. There must always be the adequate knowledge of what the Christian Faith really is. There must always be recognition of its definitiveness and its historic reality. But faith, in the Christian sense, can never be separated from the personal relationship between the believer and Jesus Christ.

Faith is not just believing certain things *about* Jesus Christ, but also believing *in* Him; and that is a matter of personal relationship. The emotions and all manner of the inner depths of human make-up are involved in this aspect of faith. We shall not be content just to be champions of orthodoxy in proclaiming the mystery of the Incarnation as opposed to humanistic or Unitarian misconceptions of our Lord's nature. We shall not be content with preaching only about Christ the King, or the Logos or the third Person of the Holy and Blessed Trinity, or the Eternal High Priest. We are to preach Christ both as God and Man, for to undervalue either aspect of His nature is heresy. To preach Christ only as God is to remove from the Gospel something of the warmth and winsomeness and personal-ness of the Faith which it was God's intention to plant and to nourish by means of His Incarnation. We are to preach Jesus of Galilee and Judea. We are to so preach faith in Jesus Christ as to include that mystical quality of warmth and rapture in human affection, that quality of confidence-of-heart which springs from mutual human love, that quality of deep, inner well-being and satisfaction flowing from companionship between persons. We are to so preach faith in Jesus Christ as to include inspiration in the presence of human greatness and goodness, and reverence and wonder in the presence of human holiness and high character.

The starting point of Christian faith historically was, in a very large sense, the response of ordinary men and women in Galilee and Judea to the enormous personal magnetism, the outreaching warmth of love and affection, and the evidences of sublime wisdom in a Man. In large measure it was of the same quality as that from which all the fabric of abiding human relations is woven. Congeniality, respect, admiration, trust, companionableness, love, and devotion were all involved in the mystery of the relationship between Jesus and those people among whom He moved on earth.

And the same is true now as it has been all through the centuries since the Ascension. Faith in Jesus Christ, at its highest and best, always includes a large measure of warm human affection of the purest and noblest sort. Christian preaching must be shot through and through with the winsomeness of Jesus of Nazareth. Nor is the spontaneous sentiment and emotion of the hearers to be discouraged or restrained. When all of that is coupled with an equal emphasis upon the mystery of the Incarnation and the adoration of God "come down from heaven for us men and for our salvation"—that is indeed to "preach Christ" in His fullness.

We Anglicans are especially prone to be a little

too reticent and reserved when it comes to the emotional content of the Christian Faith; we seem to find it difficult to talk about. We are accustomed to dignity and decorum in our liturgical worship; we are accustomed to allowing the Prayer Book and the Hymnal to speak our deepest feelings; we are rightfully suspicious of the unrestrained emotionalism which is often substituted for intellectual integrity and even for good taste among some Christian groups. All that is good, but only so long as it does not choke off or stifle a right and proper inclusion of the emotional content of the Christian's relationship to his Lord and Saviour. I suspect that the people in the pews are often much more eager to hear expressed in preaching some evidences of that emotional content than many of us preachers are prepared to voice. I do not believe that I need to hedge or to qualify an appeal for more expression of emotion in the pulpits of our Church; our inhibitions are strongly enough entrenched to prevent any possibility of kicking over the traces. And I am deeply in earnest in this admonition to put more feeling and warmth into preaching Christ. To fail to do so is a tragic shortcoming. There is a great difference between sentiment and sentimentalism; to shy

away from sentiment in order to avoid sentimentalism is a serious and senseless blunder.

There is a lovely and moving story in a book
entitled *Beside the Bonnie Brier Bush*, by Ian
Maclaren, about a young Scottish minister just
graduated from theological school. As the story begins he is in the throes of preparing his sermon for
the next day, which will be the first Sunday in the
pulpit of his little "free kirk" in a typical rural
community of Scotland. He is tremendously and
conscientiously concerned with this first facing
from the pulpit the flock committed to his care.
Nor is he unmindful that they have a right to expect much of a dominie who has just won the
MacWhammel Scholarship. So he worked far
into the night to produce a sermon that would as-
sure his people of the extent and thoroughness of
his theological training. At length he was finished
and went to inform his aunt, who kept house for
him, that he was ready for the morrow. She was
a very devout but illiterate old lady, full of warm
affection for her nephew and pride in his calling.
She said: "You'll say what's right, no doubt o'
that and a'body'll be pleased with ye. But oh,
laddie, be sure to say a guid word for Jesus."

To "say a guid word for Jesus" had been a

phrase his mother had often used in talking to him about preaching, before she died. His aunt had remembered and he had forgotten. What these simple women meant he knew full well, and he also knew now that he had forgotten. So upstairs he went, and with anguish in his soul he put the sermon in the fire and started all over again, this time to prepare one which would "say a guid word for Jesus."

The story brings home with great charm and authority the central importance of Jesus in Christian faith and Christian preaching. Its emphasis is upon the universal winsomeness and appeal of Jesus to be loved and adored, and that must never be very far from the center of our attention in preaching.

When we become aware of people's floundering in intellectual problems about religion, it is well to encourage bypassing these problems for the time being and turn their attention to the beauty and strength and attractiveness of the life and character of the Man of Galilee. After that, one can return to the problems with a new perspective and a new vision.

In the face of the profound and astonishing affirmations of Christian theology, people often cry impatiently, "Give us the simple Jesus and leave out all the complications and confusion of dogma with which He has come to be obscured." Very often this is nothing more than the reiteration of a cliché (and it is a cliché) whereby people seek to rebuke the Church and to justify their mental inertia and religious illiteracy. But sometimes this represents a degree of honest confusion and a genuine need for help. We are to give "the simple Jesus" to people. And we are to remind them in our preaching that this same Jesus gave rise to all the theology concerning Him. Tell the people that theology is no smoke-screen cast about Him by malevolent priests and popes, but rather the honest and humble effort of devout men to explain that which demands explanation. Point out to them how impossible it is to contemplate the life and character of Jesus, to study what He did and said, without becoming increasingly aware of a mystery and a profundity about Him which is satisfied by no superficial answers. The more one seeks to know of Him the less simple He appears.

Furthermore, there is always to be reckoned with that mystical something which happens within the person who turns to study and to contemplate Jesus with any degree of honest receptiveness to the truth. He becomes aware of the fact that there is a Presence beside him, the effect of which is utterly different from anything remotely comparable in the study and contemplation of great men of history.

In preaching Jesus as both Man and God it makes little difference where one starts. Begin with God, the Father, in His love, moving into time and space in the form of man to redeem His sick and wayward creation. Then show Him there in the manger and in the carpenter shop and on the shores of the Sea of Galilee and on the highways to Samaria and Jerusalem and in the temple and at the Roman Court and before the Sanhedrin and upon the Cross. Show Him in the garden of Joseph of Arimathea and on the road to Emmaus and in the Upper Room. And show how blessed and glorious it is that, having ascended to Heaven, He remains the eternal and still-present answer to the question: What is God like?

Or begin with Jesus in the flesh. Tell how He moved and captivated those people who followed Him. Tell how He healed and forgave and enlightened the sick, the sinners, and the benighted. Tell of His undiscourageable good will, His ever-ready compassion, His sublime moral beauty, His joy in the simple, everyday things of the creation, His unqualified love for all His human brethren —men, women, and children. Tell of the words He spoke revealing an unparalleled and timeless wisdom. Tell of His utter faith in God and His constant sense of divine companionship. Tell how He died and how He rose again. The more you tell, the more your listeners will be moved to seek to know more of Him and the more ready they will be for the mystical experience which leads to calling Him Lord. Tell them how His disciples failed to understand Him or to recognize Him for what He was. Tell them how it was only at long last that they began to see and to perceive.

Tell them how the light broke in St. Peter's life. Tell them of that breath-taking experience when, at Caesarea Philippi, Peter was given the vision of God in Jesus Christ. It is tremendously important to read that great passage as it should be read. I have heard it read as though Peter's answer to the question "Whom do ye say that I am?" was as matter-of-fact as the most ordinary of remarks. It could not have been other than a statement so overwhelming, so astonishing, and so wonderful for Peter as to have reduced him to trembling incredulity as he breathed this expression of the light vouchsafed him: "Thou art the Christ, the Son of the Living God!" And Jesus said to him, "Flesh and blood hath not revealed this unto thee but my Father in Heaven." And we remember St. Paul's words: "No man can say that Jesus is Lord save by the Holy Spirit." And from those words we gain fresh understanding and conviction concerning the "given-ness" of faith in Christ. For in the last analysis, our choice and decision and self-commitment can take us only so far; beyond that, we must rely upon God to give us the deeper perceptions and higher insights and fuller assurance which alone bring faith to full flowering.

In preaching Christ, we shall find the Hymnal to be richly suggestive of the wide range of experience in men's relationship and approach to Him. The Christmas hymns are especially interesting in this respect, and we do well to make use of all that we find there. From the very personal carols

Away in a manger, no crib for his bed,
The little Lord Jesus laid down his sweet head.

and

What child is this, who, laid to rest,
On Mary's lap is sleeping?

to the magnificent summary of the Incarnation in
"Hark! the Herald Angels Sing"

> Christ, by highest heaven adored;
> Christ, the everlasting Lord;
> Late in time behold him come,
> Offspring of the Virgin's womb.
> Veiled in flesh the Godhead see;
> Hail the Incarnate Deity.

there is a range of emotion and a reality of experience which is a good guide for us in preventing
our preaching from becoming too restricted and
too stereotyped.

Such hymns as

> Jesus, the very thought of thee
> With sweetness fills the breast.

and

> How sweet the Name of Jesus sounds
> In a believer's ear!
> It soothes our sorrows, heals our wounds,
> And drives away our fear.

and

> Jesus! Name of wondrous love!
> Name all other names above!
> Unto which must every knee
> Bow in deep humility.

are full of an emotional content that is genuine, and they are expressions of real piety, not just hyperbole and sentimentalism. And what a great range of emphasis and of experience is suggested as one turns from these hymns to the majestic and stirring words of

> Crown him with many crowns,
> The Lamb upon his throne.

and

> All hail the power of Jesus' Name!
> Let angels prostrate fall.

Again, what a range of emphasis and significance is revealed by

> Jesus, Lover of my soul,
> Let me to thy bosom fly.

and

> See the Conqueror mounts in triumph;
> See the King in royal state,
> Riding on the clouds, his chariot,
> To his heavenly palace gate!

If your preaching centers in Him and touches only the smallest portion of the unsearchable riches of Christ, it will be filled with a power and an attraction that will indeed move and save men's souls. If your preaching ever wanes in depth or interest, if your preparation and delivery of sermons ever lose their excitement and joy for you, if your people grow restless or indifferent, go back to Him! Study Him, meditate upon Him, adore Him, pray to Him, read and re-read His words, examine and re-examine everything He did, every relationship with people, every attitude and decision He made as revealed in the Gospels. Think long and gratefully upon what He means to you, why you love Him and why you serve Him. You will find that a new life and a new power and a new dimension come to your preaching, while you discover, simultaneously, that you have regained a new zest and a new zeal in the doing of it.

Go back again and again to such great passages of the Bible as these, and let their message permeate your preaching:

[Christ] is the image of the invisible God, the first-born of all creation; for in him all things were created, in heaven and on earth, visible and invisible, whether thrones or dominions or principalities or authorities—all things were created through him and for him. He is before all things, and in him all things hold together. He is the head

of the body, the church; he is the beginning, the
first-born from the dead, that in everything he
might be preëminent. For in him all the fullness
of God was pleased to dwell, and through him to
reconcile to himself all things, whether on earth
or in heaven. . . .

[Let Christ] dwell in your hearts through faith;
that you, being rooted and grounded in love, may
have power to comprehend with all the saints what
is the breadth and length and height and depth,
and to know the love of Christ which surpasses
knowledge, that you may be filled with all the
fullness of God.

God hath highly exalted him and bestowed on
him the Name which is above every name, that at
the Name of Jesus every knee should bow in heaven
an on earth and under the earth and every tongue
confess that Jesus Christ is Lord to the Glory of
God the Father.

I am the resurrection and the life. . . .

I am the true vine . . . you the branches.

I am the good shepherd. . . .

I am the bread of life. . . .

I am the way, and the truth, and the life. . . .

He who has seen me has seen the Father. . . .

Preach Him, and you preach the Gospel indeed!

6

"And Him Crucified"

ALL CHRISTIAN preaching must be permeated with the mysterious light of the message of the Cross. The more we preach Christ crucified, the more surely shall we keep in sight the heart of the Gospel and the clearer will be the light which shines from the Cross as our beacon in the darkness of sin and pain and perplexity. It is all too easy for preacher and people alike to fall into the way of hovering about the periphery of the Faith, for the message of the Cross is difficult. Its mystery clashes with man's pride of intellect and with his desire to cut everything down to size so that he may be master of all he surveys. It runs head-on into man's persistent attempt to escape the hard realities of life and find refuge in sentimentality; it shocks and offends man's self-love and conceit.

Before a man can discover the reassurance and inspiration and glory of the message of the Cross,

he must go through the profoundly shocking experience of its indictment and condemnation of
himself. Indeed, it is a difficult message to proclaim or to hear, and it is very understandable
why we prefer, or are easily tempted, to skirt it.
The Cross is an offense to unredeemed human
nature. It always will be, as it always has been
since our Lord Himself said on the eve of His
Crucifixion, "This day shall ye be offended because of me" (K.J.V.).

The threat of sentimentality in the attitudes
and thinking of Christian people is an especially
oppressive one. Certainly the preaching of the
Cross is an antidote for that. It is only human to
shrink from pain and hardship and the fearsome
aspects of life. It is only human to seek refuge in
a border-line world of fantasy where all is sweet
and lovely; especially in religion do people seem
to suppose this the desirable thing to do. The
Communist accusation that religion is the opiate
of the masses is not without foundation if one
were to judge on the grounds of much popular
behavior and speaking.

People are ready enough to rhapsodize about
the beauty and gentleness of the scene in Beth-
lehem's stable and to weep with sweet emotion in

contemplating the blessed Babe in His mother's arms. People are ready enough to adore the meek and gentle Jesus in His works of mercy and compassion as He moves through the countryside of Galilee and Judea. It is obvious that people find it delightful and rewarding to go to church on Easter morning to worship a risen Lord who offers them the hope and promise of eternal life. It is popular to sing praises to Christ the King enthroned in glory at the right hand of God the Father. All that is good and constructive, as far as it goes, both as behavior for all Christian disciples and as subject material for the preacher. But it is indeed another matter to be required to look upon the Son of God in agony and bloody sweat upon the Cross of Calvary; it is another matter to have thrust before us the mystery of a suffering, dying God who is compelled to endure this shame and indignity because of human sin and disobedience in which we all share the guilt.

Unless the preaching of the Gospel in all its lovelier and more gentle aspects is constantly related to and brought back to the Cross, it will be a sentimentalized distortion of Christianity. The Cross saves us from the anesthetic of sentimentality. The Cross gives our Faith a virility and sinew of which we must not be robbed. The Cross makes our Faith everlastingly relevant to life as it is, with all its inescapable, stark tragedy and with all its pain and tribulation and discipline. But far from making the Faith gloomy and dismal, as some claim, the Cross gives it glory and power and reality. Our Faith proclaims its message of hope and confidence and victory from the midst of, and in spite of, the worst that life can offer. So long as the Cross is set in our midst, none can say with any justification that our Faith is wishful thinking or blinking the facts or sugar-coating the pill. And so long as we persist in turning to the Cross and making a place for it in all our attitudes and convictions, we shall be saved from the suffocating influence of sentimentality. The Cross reveals the fact that the ever-present pain and suffering of this life is not just an alien intrusion but a source and impetus of spiritual values. It redeems the tragedy of pain and suffering from footlessness and gives it a positive place in the scheme of things.

Hosts of people have at one time or another turned away in disgust from the ghastly caricature of the Christian Faith which results from diluting or distorting the authentic, historic message of the Cross and which leaves the Gospel little more than a wishy-washy kind of moralizing with a degree of hero-worship and makes of the Church a club for the eminently respectable, whose members are meant to do social work of certain kinds and to use their influence with legislators for the general "improvement" of social and economic conditions. From such a caricature much contemplation of the Cross and its message will save us.

Christianity tells us that the Cross is the price of sin. It proclaims that on Calvary we see human sin crucifying and murdering God. And before we can even begin to gain any understanding of the Christian message that there also on the Cross is God redeeming us from the power of sin by His dying, we must preach the reality of sin and our desperate involvement in it to a generation all too insistent that sin is not very bad after all.

Living as we do in the backwash of liberalism, we hear it said, even from some pulpits which claim to be Christian, that sin is only "missing the mark," that the traditional Christian's insistence upon the awfulness of sin is just old-fashioned crepe-hanging, just an evolutionary hangover from an unenlightened age. We hear frequent accusations that the Episcopal Church is hopelessly out of step with the times in her preoccupation with the subject of sin and her insistence upon including the General Confession in her services, wherein people are required to call themselves miserable offenders with no health in them. There is a kind of nauseating complacency and blindness extant in our society, and even our Churchpeople are not altogether uninfected by it.

In a recent issue of *Parents' Magazine*, I came across the following paragraph:

> Generations of parents have assumed that babies are born with selfish, destructive instincts. They have believed that children are endowed by nature with a tendency to evil which can gain ascendancy over their better natures unless curbed. Modern psychology says this is not true. Many studies of newborn infants and young children lend no support whatever to the ancient notion that children are born with an evil bent toward selfishness and aggression.

In this ridiculous and ignorant attempt to repudiate a fundamental Christian doctrine, the writer merely adds to the ineptitude and confusion of modern thinking. The tragic aspect of it is in the suspicion that many a parent, professing Christianity, will read it and agree with it, in the belief that agreement is an indication of intellectual emancipation. The article comes to this triumphant conclusion:

When adults generally are no longer afraid to trust their children's natural dispositions, the role of parenthood will cease to be predominantly one of discipline.

My own experience has convinced me that the objective hoped for and advocated by the writer is already achieved to a dangerous extent and that the resulting maladjustment to life in the children from such homes makes them centers of infection from which all manner of maladies spread throughout society.

In the face of all that kind of thing, we preachers are called to proclaim the Christian insistence that sin is not just a smudge on the surface of life, to be erased by an indulgent God at no cost to anyone. We are to proclaim that sin scores deep and bitter furrows in the soil of life, that its consequences are devastating beyond our power to comprehend fully, that it is a brutal, diabolical slave-master before which man alone is helpless. Sin, according to Christianity, is an enlistment in the army of the powers of Evil, a defiance of and persecution of God Himself. We are to proclaim that humanity can do nought but flounder and sink farther into a morass of self-delusion and futility until we recognize that the real enemy is neither ignorance, nor stupidity, nor a defective social order, nor the crime wave, nor the liquor traffic, nor political shenanigans, nor Communism, nor war, but something deeper and more dangerous than all these things and which is itself the source and origin of them all—namely, sin, which is human defiance and disregard of God.

We must teach that sin is basically self-centeredness and self-assertiveness in all its forms; that it is self-pride and self-righteousness and self-seeking and self-sufficiency; that it is egocentricity in all its myriad forms and with all its poisonous consequences. In its toils every one of us is enmeshed, and to the oppressiveness of this dread incubus every one of us contributes. People must be led to face and to acknowledge the reality of this situation until they cry out, with St. Paul, "Who will deliver me from this body of death?" We are to do all within our power to re-establish the "ancient notion" so scathingly referred to in the article quoted, that children *are* born with an evil bent toward selfishness and aggression, with selfish and destructive instincts, and endowed by nature with a tendency to evil which can gain ascendancy over their better natures unless curbed. We are to point out something of the overwhelming evidence in human history of the ascendancy gained over better nature by the tendency to evil and the awful results of it when uncurbed. For it is not until a man's eyes have been opened to the truth of all this that he can recognize his need for salvation and be ready to experience the wonder of Christ's redeeming sacrifice for him.

People must be helped by every means possible to see beyond the shallow and treacherous claims of some modern theories of mental therapy that "what a man doesn't know won't hurt him." Over against that kind of superficiality the Christian Religion proclaims that the surest road to utter destruction is to refuse to acknowledge the dread reality of sin and to turn away from accepting the power to redeem which flows from the Cross and which God offers freely and lovingly to all who will receive it.

Certainly in preaching Christ crucified we must proclaim the *facts* of the Christian doctrine of the Atonement. I am sure there are hosts of church-going people who have only the foggiest notion as to what that doctrine is. You cannot exhort people to have faith in something if they don't know what it is. You cannot attempt the interpretation or clarifying of any doctrine as it applies to particular aspects of life until the facts of the doctrine are known first. As preachers, we must affirm the objective fact of the Christian Revelation that the Crucifixion of Jesus is God Himself performing a mighty act of redemption in history. Here is God breaking into time and space to do that for humanity which only God can do and without which mankind would be hopelessly lost. Jesus on the Cross is God in action. It is not a matter of saying, "Here is a beautiful, lofty, and moving example of goodness and courage, triumphing over cruelty and evil. Look at it. Then go and be better." It is not a matter of saying, "Here is pathos and injustice and meanness at their height. Look at it, be ashamed, and be kinder as a consequence."

The idea of "moral influence" is inescapable, to be sure; but if we think or preach it as the main significance of the Crucifixion, we are a far cry indeed from the authentic, historic message of the Cross as it has been proclaimed through the ages and as it has, from the beginning, profoundly affected and altered human life at its foundation.

We must guard against and repudiate the tendency to "modernize" the message of the Cross. The persistent attempt to dilute it, to rationalize it, to make it palatable to the onlooking secularist must be denied. It has been fashionable for a long time, as a result of the "liberal movement," to insist that "ancient propitiatory theories" are obsolete. In the face of this, the Book of Common Prayer has been an anchor to windward for which we are profoundly grateful. Its liturgy maintains the doctrine of the Atonement in all its purity and power and profundity.

There on the Cross, God takes into Himself the consequences of human sin, absorbs the cost involved, pays the price exacted, and liberates humanity. God alone is great enough and good enough to take the consequences, to absorb the cost, and to pay the price of human sin in a creation which is governed by moral law. Violated moral law demands appeasement. It cannot be violated with impunity. And therefore the Cross is the only way open to a God who is at once perfect justice and perfect love. That is the mystery of Christ, "the Propitiation for our sins," who "made there (by his one oblation of himself once offered) a full, perfect, and sufficient sacrifice, oblation, and satisfaction, for the sins of the whole world."

Nor shall we fail to declare to our people what Bishop Nygren, in *The Gospel of God*, calls the "cosmic dimensions" of our salvation by Christ. It is more than just Christ's death for you and me. Something happened to the world; it could never be the same again. There was a conquest of the powers of evil and a defeat of the Prince of Darkness to a degree which changed the nature of the bondage to which man had been subject. At the same time, while recognizing this cosmic dimension of a mighty divine act once done, there is still to be recognized the timelessness of the Atonement. Its results are yet to be fulfilled. God's suffering for us because of our sins continues; what was indeed an historic event is at the same time a continuing action.

Of course it is mysterious. Anything having to do with the nature of the Almighty, Eternal God is inescapably mysterious. It is not ours to attempt the obviously impossible task of making simple what is by nature profound. Nor is it ours to usurp the place of theologians whose minds surpass and whose training exceeds by far the abilities of us ordinary priests and preachers. Ours is to proclaim the facts of the doctrine of the Atonement and the necessity for participating in its benefits by faith and the glory in human life of the results of that faith.

The story is told of the Cardinal Archbishop of Paris, preaching in Notre Dame Cathedral on Good Friday. He recounted the story of three boys who, out of pure deviltry, decided to make false confessions, which is a grave form of blasphemy. The priest to whom they went was a wise and godly man. He soon became aware of what was happening. Instead of becoming angry, he quietly and compellingly assigned penance to the boys. "Go out there in the church," he commanded. "Kneel down before the Crucifix and say ten times, 'God did that for me and I don't care a snap of the fingers.' " "My dear people," said the archbishop, with the tears running down his cheeks, "I was one of those boys. And I learned the profoundly moving lesson, in a way never to be forgotten, that a human soul cannot look directly at Him on the Cross and say, 'I do not care.' "

Just as something happened *for* us men and for our salvation when Christ died on the Cross—something of cosmic significance which benefits all humanity whether it knows it or not, whether it acknowledges it or not—so does something more happen *to* a man when he contemplates the Cross, when he reaches out to appropriate by faith the blessings of the Cross, when he commits himself by willing choice to follow and to adore Jesus Christ as Lord and Saviour and can affirm with humble, passionate gratitude, "Jesus died for me."

This has been universally characteristic of all Christian experience, and our whole Christian heritage is highly charged with witness to this experience. Here again we find the Hymnal to be a rich source of evidence for this central aspect of Christian experience, expressed in verse which is always one of the best media for profound and mystic aspects of truth. We must teach our people to meditate carefully upon the significance of such familiar hymns as "When I survey the wondrous Cross" and "In the Cross of Christ I glory" and "Beneath the Cross of Jesus." Make plain to your people that such hymns are not poetic exaggerations and flights of literary hyperbole, but rather the expressions of real and deep experience and insight on the part of ordinary Christian people, the classic content of which is to be a part of every Christian's life.

Of all our heritage in the Hymnal, could there be any verse to surpass the third stanza of Paulus

Gerhardt's "O sacred head, sore wounded," with which to close this chapter?

> In thy most bitter passion
>   My heart to share doth cry,
> With thee for my salvation
>   Upon the cross to die.
> Ah, keep my heart thus movèd
>   To stand thy cross beneath,
> To mourn thee, well-belovèd,
>   Yet thank thee for thy death.

7

Know What You Have to Say

IN PREPARING to preach, the first thing necessary is to know what you are going to say. The last thing necessary, before you may consider yourself ready to preach, is to have so prepared your material that the people will know what you had to say when you get through. The old story about the successful preacher who diagnosed his effectiveness by explaining that he began by telling the people what he was going to say, then said it, then told them what he had said, is one which can be pondered and remembered to good effect by every preacher.

Another story, familiar enough to be threadbare, is nonetheless significant enough to be retold. President Calvin Coolidge, the acme of reticence, went to church one Sunday alone. Upon his return, his wife, Grace, asked him what the sermon was about.

"Sin," he replied.

Unsatisfied, she pursued the matter, "Well, what did he say about sin?"

"He was against it," said Calvin.

The point I want to make is that Mr. Coolidge, in his terse remarks, may very well have exhausted his knowledge of what was said, rather than simply have been "holding out" on his wife. And furthermore, he may have had a much clearer and more comprehensive knowledge of what was said in that sermon than ninety-nine out of a hundred other members of the congregation. What is told as an anecdote illustrative of Coolidge's taciturnity could be regarded, were all the facts known, as an indication of his perspicacity in finding one positive idea in the midst of what was to most listeners a smog of words.

At first glance it may appear too elementary and obvious even to mention that a preacher must know what he is going to say before he begins. Yet my own experience leads me to believe that not to know is one of the commonest failings of preachers. If you cannot write down in one coherent and reasonably brief sentence what you intend to say, then you are not ready to begin writing your sermon. If you do not write down at the very beginning what you are going to say in one coherent and reasonably brief sentence, then you are making the whole thing much more difficult for yourself and for your congregation than is necessary or sensible. I believe that there is no one idea or recommendation which is more important, more helpful, and more conducive to effective preaching than this: Require of yourself, with rigid and unswerving discipline, that before you begin to preach you write down in one coherent, reasonably brief sentence what you are going to say!

Do not try to proceed until that has been done. And having done it, be entirely satisfied that the content of the sentence is of enough significance to justify a sermon. Having written the sentence, keep referring back to it as you proceed in developing the sermon. This is invaluable in the avoidance of irrelevant meanderings away from the subject. Ruthlessly eliminate anything which wanders from the heart of what you want to say, no matter how eloquent and effective it sounds in its own right.

You must also remember without ceasing and without question that the effectiveness of your sermons can never be properly evaluated by the standards of your own judgment or your own personal satisfaction. The proof of the pudding is in the eating, and since a sermon is not an end in itself, nor primarily a work of literary art nor an intellectually impregnable treatise to be dissected and diagnosed by experts, its excellence and value are to be determined in greatest measure by what the people "take home" with them. Whether or not you think the sermon was good is not really important. Nor, for that matter, is it important whether or not your people think it is good. The really important question is, Did you convey to them something definite enough and memorable enough to take root?

If people do not understand your sermons you will do better not to consider that a reflection upon their capacity or their intelligence, but rather upon your effectiveness as a preacher. This is not to be considered in any way a qualification of the necessity to avoid trying above all to please or divert your people, nor does this create a conflict with the earlier warning against preaching for applause and approval; those must remain pitfalls of the most serious nature. What you have to say must be evaluated on the basis of whether or not, when you get through, your people know what you had to say; the effectiveness of how you say it must be determined by whether or not your people can remember it the next day. And it is up to you to be alert to these reactions, which will come to your attention in many ways, so that you may alter and adjust your techniques and methods as often and as much as is necessary.

You are not preparing legal briefs when you prepare sermons. You are not trying a case before a court when you preach. You are not dealing with a shrewd and hostile prosecuting attorney or counsel for the defense. You need not include in every sermon all the material which can be unearthed by rigorous research on the subject under consideration. You do not present every side of a question in each sermon. Many a good sermon has been ruined by tacking on a second sermon introduced by such phrases as "But on the other hand . . ." or "At the same time we must recognize . . ." This danger can be avoided most effectively by the suggested writing out of a concise topical sentence at the start of one's preparation. It is a special characteristic of beginners to put in each sermon far too much material, and it is a failing not always outgrown by experience. It is better to preach unconventionally short and concise sermons than to proceed as though there were a law requiring the "filling up" of fifteen or twenty minutes.

Your listeners are on your side to begin with, ninety per cent of the time. Indeed, no one ever faces an audience under any other circumstances with as much favorable bias toward the speaker at the beginning. The patience and forebearance of churchgoing people is, on the whole, remarkable when one considers what they have to put up with in us preachers. It is always with reluctance that members of a congregation come to the conclusion that their rector is not much of a preacher. It is with disappointment and certain inner misgivings that some of them begin to stay away and to drift into bad habits about churchgoing because of the poor preaching. And no matter how poor it is, some never stop going, which is one of the great evidences of the divine nature of the Church and of the great depth of genuine piety in the souls of Christian people. Yes, you have a situation to begin with which is wonderfully heartening. And if a deliberate effort is made, by means of sermons on preaching and sermons on heeding, to deepen, to expand, and to stimulate that inherent receptiveness and that incipient faith in the significance of what is going on, the results will be better than one would feel he had a right to expect.

Since there is little, if any, hostility to begin

with, a preacher may and must avoid with diligence any tendency to become contentious or argumentative in the pulpit. It is often true that there are no questions or misgivings on the part of a congregation in regard to some particular subject until the preacher raises them. Sometimes it is necessary to raise misgivings and questions about certain conventional attitudes, certain fashionable misconceptions, certain comfortable clichés. But be sure to put positive and clearly-defined ideas and thoughts in the place of those which might have been undermined or opened to question. It has been said of one great preacher that "he established more than he destroyed," and that ought to be something that could be said of every preacher.

There is a tendency in us all to diagnose rather than to prescribe. It seems to be easier to point out the errors, the weaknesses, the shortcomings, the ominous signs and threats of worse to come in human society and in the lives of individuals than it is to show clearly how the power of the Christian Gospel can be brought to bear upon each situation and difficulty. People by and large, if they are at all alert to the conditions of the world and of human life in general, need no preacher to tell them that there is cause for deep concern and for grave fears. Most people nowadays are haunted with the most disturbing misgivings and with the most dismal forebodings. This is often called—and accurately, I believe—an age of harrying fears. It is for preachers of the Christian Gospel to establish the grounds upon which the human spirit may find security in the midst of life's maelstrom. Their message will be characterized by the words "We will not fear, though the earth be moved, and though the hills be carried into the midst of the sea; Though the waters thereof rage and swell, and though the mountains shake at the tempest of the same" (Great Bible). The preacher will speak with his lips and show forth in his life and demonstrate with the obvious depth and vitality of his own faith that "neither death, nor life, nor angels, nor principalities, nor powers, nor things present, nor things to come, nor height, nor depth, nor any other creature, shall be able to separate us from the love of God, which is in Christ Jesus our Lord" (K.J.V.).

We do best, you see, when we preach out of the reality of our own personal conviction and experience. The preacher must not only know what he has to say but what he has to say must be known by him through very personal experience and conviction. To preach out of a book may sound wonderfully erudite, and the subject-matter may be entirely true; it is a temptation which presses with peculiar force upon the beginner whose experience is as yet very limited. But the difference between preaching from one's own personal experience and preaching out of a book is as obvious to a congregation as a sore thumb. They may not be able to diagnose or to express in words this distinction which is so obvious. But it will be nonetheless unmistakable and they will sense it in their hearts. That which comes out of actual personal experience, even though elementary and immature, evokes a warmth of response from, and gives clearness of light to, the listeners which no second-hand ideas could possibly match even if the source represents the heights of greatness and truth.

There is an old saying that "all work and no plagiarism makes Jack-in-the-pulpit a dull boy." And there is much telling truth in the saying. Plagiarism, in its least obnoxious meaning, is to pass on to people the wisdom and experience of others; but first it must be absorbed and digested and related to your own experience. Constantly before you must be the question, "What does this mean to me?" That is true of the Gospel itself. The great concepts of Christianity must be studied and contemplated and dwelt upon in one's own heart and mind until one can answer clearly, if not profoundly, What does this mean to me? It should be obvious that you cannot make real and alive to your listeners what is not real and alive to you. Having limited ourselves to speaking "that which we do know for ourselves," we then proceed to set it in the framework of the great classical concepts of the Revealed Gospel.

Reference to oneself and one's own experience can be overdone very easily. Too frequent use of the word "I" is to be avoided. That is axiomatic and every lecturer on preaching includes it in his admonitions. Yet I am satisfied that there is no need to be extreme in this matter. I believe that some use of one's own experience, referred to as such, is desirable. Certainly when you refer to subjects like sin and willfulness and human weakness, you will do well to let your people know that your knowledge of such matters is based very much upon the difficulties you have with yourself. And when you speak of salvation and grace, put the emphasis upon your own sense of need and upon your own depth of gratitude for the availability and possession of such blessings. When you speak of Jesus, let it be evident how dear He is to you and that your emotions are involved as well as your intellect in believing the doctrine of the Incarnation.

Let your people know that you and they alike are in process of growth and development in the Christian life. You are not an authority nor are you to permit them to suppose you are. You and they alike are under authority and that authority is the authority of the Gospel itself. You do not know all the answers and it is fatal to give the impression that you do. You are subject to the same bewilderments and perplexities which assail them. The mysteries of pain and sorrow and death and evil press upon you with the same vigor as they do upon your people. Mystery is to be freely acknowledged by the preacher. And you are to give them the answers that you are able to give yourself—based on the authority of the Gospel, not on your own. Admit freely your own difficulties and point out to your people that your only recourse is the Gospel which is also theirs. It is not your answers but the Gospel's answers that you have to offer. There must always be evident in your preaching the strong note of "thus saith the Lord." He says it for the preacher, as well as for the people. Having declared what the Lord hath spoken, the preacher then goes on to tell how it applies to life's affairs as he has discovered it in his own experience. Insights and glimpses of the positive values in mystery, and confidence in the face of mystery, and acceptance of the necessity for submitting to authority when searching for light in the midst of mystery are all grist for the preacher's mill.

I remember well one of the most gratifying reactions to preaching that ever came to my attention. A man who had not been inside a church for years and who had considered the whole business of the Church as superfluous suddenly began to appear in the congregation Sunday after Sunday, as does happen, strangely enough, every once in a while. At length he was confirmed, and on Christmas following I received a small package from him. Upon opening it, I found a pair of polaroid glasses with a little note which read, "In the hope that these may help you to see more clearly on the golf course next summer as you have helped me to see more clearly in matters eternal."

No preacher could ask for more than that. Not to give all the answers, not to prove a proposition, not to explain away all difficulties, not to win a personal follower, but to help a person to see more clearly in matters eternal. That is at once our prayer and our privilege and our task. And because we are thinking about preaching as giving light, we shall turn our attention for a moment to a commonplace source of fog in preaching: the misuse of stories, anecdotes, and so-called illustrations. This is treacherous ground indeed. Not long ago I heard a certain preacher being praised in extravagant terms because he "keeps his congregation in stitches." To get laughs is an attractive objective, because it delights people and causes them to praise the preacher. And when I say people, I mean, of course, undiscriminating and unperceptive people, of whom there are always enough in any group or any congregation to mislead a preacher in his self-analysis or to throw his perspective out of kilter. To use humor properly and to elicit smiles or even an occasional laugh is right and desirable. But to keep a congregation "in stitches" is a cheapening of the Gospel to a degree bordering on blasphemy.

The treachery in the use of stories and anecdotes

is not limited to eliciting laughs. It also lies in the liking of many people for being entertained or diverted as a substitute for being enlightened. And because it pleases people, a preacher is so easily led astray in his attitudes and methods! Stories and anecdotes must be used with extreme care and most sparingly. Every one of them which is not obviously relevant and clearly enlightening must be ruthlessly eliminated no matter how good or entertaining or delightful it may be in itself. Otherwise they cheapen and becloud the holy responsibility of preaching, and make tawdry that which has its own intrinsic value and needs no garish color to dress it up.

Be sure you distinguish clearly and honestly between the comments or reactions of those whose perception and judgment are questionable and those whose understanding and appreciation are obviously deep and intelligent. Teach your people in your preaching to be perceptive and discerning. Give them a standard by which to judge the preaching of the Gospel as distinguished from entertainment with a slight religious flavor.

Know, then, what you are going to say. Be sure it is the authentic Christian Gospel and not a caricature. Say it clearly and emphatically with the authority of personal experience and great conviction. Then tell your listeners what you have said in terms of its application to life and daily habits and attitudes. Be sure it is congenial to the great affirmation, "Thus saith the Lord!" Then you will be preaching indeed.

8

How to Do It

GET A loose-leaf notebook. Have it within
reach when you are reading. Take it with
you when you are on the train. Take it to conferences, quiet days, lectures, and all occasions when
you are expecting enlightenment, suggestion, or
refreshment from others. Indeed, have it with you
just as much of the time as is practicable, for you
never know when the Spirit will move you. You
never know when your mind will suddenly begin
to race with excitement and creativeness under
some sudden stimulus. Ideas and insights come
with unpredictable caprice. In fact, our minds
and sensibilities are peculiarly rebellious under
controlled orders to come and go as we bid them.
To set aside a time for study and sermon preparation is absolutely indispensable; to neglect to do
so is inexcusable laziness or maladjustment. But
to shut one's mind and spirit at all other times or
to fail to be ready to make notes, to give actual ex-

pression in writing to unbidden and unexpected movings of the Spirit whenever they come, is to run on half your cylinders. That is indeed to grieve the Holy Spirit of God.

To start from scratch each week to prepare a sermon is to insure doing it the hard way and to insure a minimum of effective preaching. You must have many incipient sermons "cooking." Have your notebook full of pages containing but an idea or two on each. Have numbers of topical sentences written across the tops of otherwise blank pages. As you read, you will have frequent impulses to turn to one of those pages and fill some of the space. You will have similar impulses at very inopportune moments. Sometimes you will get out of bed and grope your way in the darkness to your desk so that you can get down in writing a captive idea or insight before it escapes you. Following personal counseling and interviews you will seize the ever-present notebook. In the middle of a service—perhaps while reading the Epistle or the Gospel or a Psalm or a familiar collect— an insight or a new understanding will come, and, if you are wise, you will hurry immediately after the service to imprison the idea in writing.

When you have written down these things that

may some day be sermons, you will have planted a seed in your mind as well as in your notebook. And this seed germinates in ever so many instances quite unnoticed by you. Of course, many seeds will die before any roots have taken hold; but enough will sprout to make the effort and the discipline amply rewarding.

In this whole business, we must learn the patience of those who work in the soil. We are laborers in God's vineyard. We are workers in His harvest. How often it was that our Lord used for illustrations of His message the ways of nature in the soil, in the seed, in the fields, in all growing things! And those whose lives depend immediately upon the processes of nature can teach us the value and wisdom of patient waiting and dependence upon higher powers over which we have no control. The land must be prepared, the seed must be planted, the soil must be cultivated and cared for incessantly. But germination and growth are of God. No man can create or produce the forces which bring to fruition.

So it is in preaching and in all the ministry of Word and Sacrament. We plant the seed, we nourish the soil, we struggle with weeds, we cultivate in every way we know. Then we pray for the rain and the sunshine and the mysterious creative forces which produce life and harvest-time. We cannot unnaturally hasten the processes; we cannot substitute our skill and wisdom nor our time schedule for that which must come from outside and above us. The patience and resignation and trust of the farmer must be ours if we would be laborers in His harvest and His vineyard, laborers worthy of our hire and laborers together with Him. You are to keep the soil of your mind and heart receptive and cultivated at all times, and toward that end your notebook will be of great value.

As you move nearer to the actual preaching of a sermon which has been germinating, or sprouting, for some time, write and write and write. Make rough drafts into semi-rough drafts, and semi-rough drafts into final drafts. Every time you write it over, you will discover new opportunities for saying it just the way it ought to be said, and new insights and new "slants" will come to you.

And that brings us to the consideration of manuscripts. In reading a large number of books on preaching, and hearing many lectures on the subject, I find almost unanimous agreement among the best that no one is ready to preach until he has written out, word for word, what he is going to say. It is a discipline which is evaded at the expense of effectiveness. It is a requirement which is side-stepped at the cost of not doing one's best. It is an exacting duty which is denied only at a price of lowered conscientious principle.

As to whether or not the manuscript is to be taken into the pulpit is another question. I happen to believe that there are very, very few preachers gifted enough to preach without a manuscript in the pulpit. I have come to that conclusion at the cost of a good many aggregate hours of intense irritation and bitter disappointment and cloudy bewilderment in listening to the disorganized, vapid meanderings of preachers obviously not so gifted, who thought they were. I know it is true that the membership is very large and vocal in the school which holds that preaching without a manuscript must be done at any cost (which amounts to supposing that twaddle without a manuscript is preferable to saying something with a manuscript). But despite the large enrollment in this "school of hard knocks for the laity," I am not of it, and for what seems to me very good reason —namely, that it takes rare gifts to preach well without a manuscript and most of us do not possess those gifts. I believe the idea of "no manuscript in the pulpit at any cost" is on the decline. I certainly hope so, most earnestly, for the sake of our people and for God's sake. I recommend for those who are not geniuses of a sort (and I sincerely mean that it takes a genius of a sort to do otherwise) that you learn to *preach* from a manuscript. And I make a definite distinction between preaching from a manuscript and reading from one. You *can* learn to preach from a manuscript so that it does not necessarily get between you and your congregation.

In a sermon you must have something to say—something specific and concise. And it must be said in such a way that your people will know definitely, after you are through, what you said. You are not just filling up twenty minutes. You are not performing a stunt. You are attempting conscientiously to convey something worthwhile and enlightening from a God who seeks to use you to a people who reach out to receive it. You are not trying to establish a reputation as a virtuoso. You are not trying to impress people with your skill or your memory or your self-possession. You have something to say and to "put over," and that something is infinitely more important than yourself or your reputation.

A manuscript will serve as a firm hand to hold you in line and keep you on your course. It will be a constant reminder to you that you have a purpose to accomplish, not a feat to perform or a personal reputation to build up. It will prevent that tragic and wasteful jumping from one unrelated idea to another until your preaching is, as someone has put it, like a clothesline on which is pinned a series of variegated but unconnected articles of clothing. It will prevent that exasperating impression that preaching is only an aimless wandering from field to field, browsing a little here and ruminating a little there and resulting in having gotten exactly nowhere in particular at the end of the journey.

The right and proper use of a manuscript will also spare you the expenditure of a great deal of nervous energy and general tension as preaching time draws near—an energy which ought to be expended in much more constructive tasks than mere anticipation, and a tension which deserves a more worthy adversary than an approaching deadline.

Furthermore, the right use of a manuscript will relieve your people of two kinds of subtle torment. The first of these is the suspicion that their preacher has not prepared himself to the extent that he should, and the second is that miserable uneasiness which comes from the awareness that the speaker is not as sure as he ought to be where he is going next, and where he is going to come out, and is rather nervous about it himself. A manuscript gives confidence and peace of mind to both people and preacher.

Careful writing out of a sermon, with subsequent study and re-study of the manuscript, is like turning on a strong, pitiless searchlight which reveals in all its true shoddiness the careless use of words, the sloppy grammar, and the inept illustrations. It also reveals and makes inescapably obtrusive the fuzzy edges of ideas which have not been thought through and mastered. It brings relentlessly into view the clichés, the truisms and the words that are only words, all of which are mere "sounding brass and a tinkling cymbal." Those loose and heedless habits of speech which creep so persistently and insidiously into one's ordinary conversational use should be kept out of the pulpit. Especially in the light of the majestic and euphonious beauty of the language of the Prayer Book must we avoid the glaring contrast of uncouth and graceless speech from the pulpit. And there is no better attack upon this problem than the ruthless pruning of a sermon manuscript.

Once the hard work and the disciplined study of preparing the manuscript have been done, begin the process of learning to preach the sermon, that is, to deliver it, to "put it across." Much of this can be done in one's study or when driving between pastoral calls or just before dropping off to sleep at night or at any one of many odd times. But mostly it is learned in the process of preaching Sunday after Sunday.

"There is no substitute for experience," is almost a cliché but, like many extremely familiar remarks, it is often overlooked or belittled because of the very fact that it is so familiar. Experience is different from mere repetition. One can preach for twenty years and still do it in precisely the same way as on the very first occasion of mounting the pulpit. There must be a conscious, purposeful determination to learn and to grow. Experience is, in large measure, created and wrought out of the material of living and doing.

One must deliberately set about the business of learning to use the voice with its capacities for inflection and varied range. One must school himself in the exercise of articulation. The monot-

onous intoning of sermons can be exceeded only
by sloppy enunciation as a means of destroying utterly the effectiveness of even the very best
material and subject matter. It is really astonishing
how many preachers sound as though they have
potatoes in their mouths and who drop their voices
at the end of a sentence to such an extent that one
quickly relinquishes any attempt to follow.

Perhaps it is not out of order to tell the story of
the man who fell asleep during a sermon and as a
result tumbled into the aisle, breaking his arm.
Being very angry about it all, he went to his lawyer
to seek some possible means of redress. After careful consideration, the lawyer proposed that he sue
the preacher for having administered an anesthetic
without a license. Ridiculous though it is, let it be
a warning, for the story will not be heard without
arousing a genuine sympathy for the victim in
the hearts of many a layman.

It must be recognized and admitted that there
is a real conflict involved between being natural—
"being oneself"—and the danger of sounding
stilted, artificial, affected, or bombastic. To the
resolution of that conflict we must set our wills in
sincere determination. One can form habits of
careful articulation, flexibility of voice range, and

change of pace by persistent practice, until that becomes as natural to him as the former habits of careless, monotonous speech.

One of the outstanding examples of this aspect of the art of preaching, in my experience of hearing preachers, is Bishop Bennet of Rhode Island, recently retired. At times his words pour out in staccato style with machine-gun speed. This rouses and stirs the listener like a challenge to attention. The next moment there may be a sudden and completely unheralded pause, then a lowering of the voice in measured emphasis. Sometimes in subdued tones and then in quickly rising pitch, he comes to the making of his point with dramatic effectiveness. Yet through it all there is no trace of affectation and no appearance of professionalism. He has indeed mastered a full use of the wide potentialities in the human voice and dedicated that learned skill to the dispensing of the Word of God.

With full recognition of the variety and difference in human beings, and allowing all necessary room for diversity of native talents and capacities, one may still have a right to expect every preacher, subject only to physiological limitations, to make full use of the universal flexibility of the human voice. For it is inevitable that in preaching, *what* one says is equaled in importance by *how* one says it. In fact, it is often true that subject matter of lesser quality will, when well spoken, be more effective preaching than the best of material poorly spoken.

To be the master in some degree of an effective technique is the only way one can forget himself and be loosed from the inhibitions of self-consciousness. Of course, the ideal is to be so filled with the objective glory of the Gospel that one need never think of himself or his technique or any aspect of the mechanics of preaching. But that is a capacity with which few of us are endowed to any striking degree. And it is to theologues and to run-of-the-mill clergymen like myself that I speak. Any others must simply bear with me.

Take comfort and courage in awareness of the fact that your congregation wants to hear *you* preach and they want to know the extent of *your* conviction and the angle of *your* view on this or that aspect of the Gospel. Phillips Brooks and many others have said better and more effectively what you and I try to say in our pulpits. But our people would not be content for us to read the sermons of Phillips Brooks or of any other great preacher, no matter how well we might read them; for there is a mysterious and wonderful dimension in preaching which involves the direct contact of person with person and spirit with spirit. That is why reading books or listening to the radio can never be a satisfactory substitute for preaching. That is why, sooner or later, habitual radio listeners are going to show up in church and tell you after the service that they "had to come to see what it was really like."

Be earnest, be hard-working, be humble, be a faithful pastor, be eager and determined to grow and to develop in your ability to proclaim effectively the wonderful news of Christ. After that, you may trust God to use you and you may trust your people to be grateful for the privilege of having you as their priest and pastor and preacher.

9

"The Temper of the Times"

THE PREACHER must be well-informed and analytical concerning the temper of the times in which he lives. He must know and diagnose the fads and fancies of popular attitude and opinion. He must be familiar with the intellectual and spiritual climate in which move both the "man in the street" and the member of the intelligentsia or the "egg-head." Each has his own ethos, his own jargon, and his own clichés. Each is preoccupied with his own set of contemporary skepticisms and espoused causes.

Not only must the preacher be aware of, and familiar with, these fads and fancies of the era in which he lives, but he must also describe them and analyze them so that they may be seen in the right perspective by his people. The Christian Faith has something definite to say to all these phases of the human mind, for it has lived with them from the beginning. There are only a few really basic heresies which remain fundamentally the same from age to age, even though they crop up in various guises and are expressed in various terminologies in each particular period. People need help in understanding the moth-eaten character of the so-called "challenges to the Christian Faith" which, apart from history's perspective, are so apt to appear new and as the product of "modern advances" in learning. Once people are enabled to see these problems in the right perspective and to recognize them as old and familiar chestnuts, they can make their choices and decisions much more intelligently. To preach without studied reference to the frame of popular opinion and attitude in which is set the task in each generation is to encourage the pigeonholing of religion and the regarding of it as a kind of esthetic addendum to real life.

Ours is an age which is described on every side as secular. Not only from the occupants of pulpits but from businessmen and statesmen and military men do we hear it said repeatedly that secularism is perhaps the most immediate and destructive threat to our existence as a free people, as well as to the growth of the Church. Now, I am not at all sure that ours is any more secular than many other ages of history; I am sure secularism has always been a serious and persistent threat to the best and highest values of human life and society. It is an inevitable result of Original Sin, and that we have with us always. But be that as it may, secularism is certainly an overwhelming fact confronting us now, and the sound of the word is as familiar to all our people as any other they ever hear in connection with the task and problems of the Church. Because the word is so commonplace and because there is such general agreement as to its danger, we preachers do well to begin at the point where we are, to isolate and to define the word and its implications, to recognize it as a setting and as a background for preaching in these times. We must also recognize for ourselves and point out to our people the alarming extent to which secularism has infected the attitudes of Church people as well as of the unchurched. It is dangerous for people to be allowed to suppose that because they are Church members they are automatically beyond and outside the effect of the acids which corrode the mind and spirit of the society in which they live.

Secularism means the denial of God in practice. There is little enough denial of God in theory.

Even among our intellectuals it is now fairly respectable to profess belief in a "Higher Power." At least such a profession no longer evokes the amount of general contempt on the part of one's colleagues that it did some years ago. To be sure, Whitaker Chambers brought down upon his head a storm of abuse and contempt from his colleagues among the intelligentsia when his book was published, but I suspect it was because he went so far as to insist that religion is the only constructive alternative to, and salvation from, Communism and its by-products, rather than just the fact that he confessed to a belief in a Higher Power. His fault, in the eyes of the intellectuals, was that he came to take religion seriously: he insisted upon going beyond a theoretical belief.

Theoretical belief really makes no difference at all in the affairs of mankind, nor in the life of the individual. Nor, for that matter does theoretical denial make very much difference. Many people acknowledge God in theory and deny Him in practice. And that is basically what secularism is, at least among the people to whom we preach.

The minority who deny God both in theory *and* practice are a loudly vocal element found in our times chiefly among the academic circles associ-

ated with some of our institutions of higher learning. They will not be in the pews listening to the
preaching of the Word, but their influence is felt
in the pews, and their presence in society must be
acknowledged.

It is the denial of God *in practice* which is the
strength of the threat called secularism, just as it
is the acknowledgment of God *in practice* which
makes religion significant and vital. And our
people in this day and age need desperately to have
driven home to them the fact that theoretical
acknowledgment of God is really of no significance
whatsoever unless it is accompanied by the acceptance of the requirements to *do* certain things
at certain times in certain places in certain ways
for certain purposes. Many of our people believe
that there is great virtue and value in consenting
to belief in "the existence of a Higher Power"
without any strongly implemented relationship to
habits of worship and service. This is a far cry
indeed from belief in the God and Father of our
Lord, from self-commitment to Christ, from allegiance to the authentic Faith of the ages as set
forth in the Creed, and from showing forth the
praise of Christ "not only with our lips, but in our
lives, by giving up ourselves to [His] service

and by walking before [Him] in holiness and righteousness all our days."

I suppose one of the chief evidences of this denial of God in practice, which is secularism, is the abandonment of divine worship as a duty or, at best, the relegating of it to a place incidental and secondary to the pursuit of business, pleasure, or things, or to mere convenience. I am sure this has been a basic difficulty from the beginning of the Church, but in our day it is characterized by the stamp of approval among many "good" Church members as well as among the generally indifferent. Even among the clergy one finds to-day a deep-rooted reluctance to be explicit and firm in facing or even in acknowledging this basic illness.

To neglect or to belittle worship means to neglect and to belittle that which gives rise to worship, namely, a sense of dependence upon God for human well-being, a delight in the sense of His presence, and a realization of God's judgment as the final reality with which human life must reckon. It is irrelevant to insist, as do both people and clergy, that there are other things just as important or more important than faithful obedience of the Prayer Book injunction "to worship

God every Sunday in his Church." Everybody
grants the truth of that. But having granted it,
you are still exactly where you were. Only a fool
would claim that churchgoing is the beginning
and the end or the all-in-all of Christian discipleship. But only a blind man will allow to go un-
challenged the idea that churchgoing is just not
very important. Only a religious illiterate would
espouse the popular idea that if one "believes in a
Higher Power" and "considers himself religious
at heart," he is a good Christian despite a totally
undisciplined, flabby, and self-indulgent attitude
toward the practice of religion.

To preach about the value and importance of
churchgoing is an extremely unpopular pursuit.
Even passing references to it from the pulpit are
bound to elicit rather heated reiterations of the
old cliché about scolding people in church for
the sins of those not in church. The fact remains
glaringly apparent that only a small percentage of
any church's membership is present on any one
Sunday and that a large segment of every Sunday's
congregation is made up of people who go to
church only once in a while when it is entirely con-
venient and when there is nothing else "more interesting" to be done on that day. The reason they

don't go is because they think it is unimportant. And one reason why they think it is unimportant is because the clergy have not affirmed its importance with enough unanimity or enough conviction or enough courage. And if it is not important then the Church itself is not important, and that is precisely what hosts of people believe.

This persistent and general belittling of the importance of worship (which is a form of belittling God) is one of the chief evidences of the inroads of secularism upon society and the Church. And a determined attempt to restore a recognition of the importance of worship and the rightness of its claim upon Christian people is one of the best ways of refuting and counteracting the influence of secularism. Preach, then, on the subject of the value and meaning and importance of regular churchgoing. And do it with courage and persistence! You will often be convinced that yours is the voice of one crying in the wilderness, but the day will come when you will be vindicated.

It is easy to fall victim to the basic blunder of supposing that doubt and cynicism always come first and that from such things flows inevitably the neglect of worship which is a form of denying God in practice. I am sure it is even more true that the neglect or abandonment of worship gives rise to doubt and cynicism. It is quite as true to say, "He who worships believes" as it is to say, "He who believes worships." The surest way to destroy faith is to do nothing about it. The surest way to encourage and to renew faith is to *act* on the assumptions of faith. Our convictions and our attitudes follow upon the heels of our standards of behavior quite as much, if not more, than the other way around.

We all recognize readily enough that Communism is our implacable enemy; anything which derides truth, exalts falsehood as a virtue, regards human life as cheap, and honors slavery and mass murder is an enemy too blatant to miss. It is not so generally recognized that Communism is only secularism taken seriously and carried to its logical conclusion. The difference between Communism and secularism is one of degree rather than of kind.

Secularism as compared to Communism is like a small microbe of disease lying dormant for the time being in the bloodstream of society. Communism is an aggressive, virulent manifestation of that same microbe, multiplying with vicious speed and destroying the tissue of the body with angry purpose. Secularism may be nothing more than a kind of empty-headed, sophisticated dallying with ideas in lieu of settling down in marriage to life itself. It may be surrounded with an aura of innocence and respectability and intellectual approval. But that makes it no less lethal. The fact that our educational system is dominated by secularism causes little general concern because ours is a society which idolizes education as such. We applaud education for the sake of education without caring much what kind of education it is nor what end it aims to serve. Nonetheless, the stubborn fact remains that secularism as we know it and serve it is the same philosophy in the domesticated state that Communism is in the wild. They are horses of the same color even though one is bridled at the moment and the other is not. They are birds of the same feather even though one has almost no support from respectable people while the other has behind it all the prestige of an adulated educational system.

Another aspect of the temper of our times is the cult of toleration. This, is of course, the handmaiden of secularism. But it is a more sharply-defined attitude of mind than secularism in general and it is one which has been espoused by many people who profess Christianity as being evidence of the reality of their profession. In every congregation one comes across some people who equate Christianity with this cult of toleration. The gist of this cult's claim is this, that all opinions and beliefs are equally good no matter how utterly at odds with each other they may be.

It is difficult to know how this came to be so generally considered as peculiarly Christian. For as a matter of fact, it is essentially and utterly ridiculous. Perhaps it has been caused by the frantic efforts of respectable Church people to reconcile the religious illiteracy of their admired, if not beloved, alma maters with their cherished family church where their parents worshipped with genuine devotion and where they themselves grew up amid happily-remembered associations. It is indeed true that many people find themselves threatened with a kind of schizophrenia in attempting to be good alumni and good Christians at the same time. This cult of toleration extols "neutralism," insists that there are no absolutes, confuses open-mindedness with empty-headedness, and tolerance with spinelessness. All of which contributes to producing the unbelievably fantastic situation of a person's supposing the chief evidence

of his Christian faith to be in his insistence that
Judaism and Taoism and every other religion are
equally good and true.

With all this the preacher must deal. He must
help his people to diagnose these confusions and
misconceptions for themselves, so that the presentation of the proper Christian view will do more
than bounce off the armor of preconceived preju-
dices and hopelessly muddle-headed confusion. He
is to help them see and preserve the positive values
which lie at the core of these confusions, lest they
be forced to reject the truth as a person with serious indigestion must of necessity reject another
morsel of food no matter how good and nutritious
it may be.

There certainly is great need for putting straight
the popular ideas of tolerance. True tolerance is
respect for the right of another to believe as he
chooses while all the time you are convinced with
all your heart and mind that he is deeply and
dangerously wrong. Tolerance does not require
that you agree with every opinion and belief in
the world. To defend another's right to believe
differently from yourself when you are either
not sure what you do believe or not sure that what

you believe is right is not tolerance at all; it is just addlepated neutralism.

True tolerance demands that no man be persecuted because of his beliefs even when those beliefs differ profoundly from the belief of the majority. But it certainly does not require that you turn your children over to be taught by that man nor that the man be permitted to proclaim his beliefs without challenge when they conflict with yours or when they threaten the security, well-being, and orderliness of society. To protect a man from persecution and to encourage him in destructive violence are not the same thing. To permit a man to believe what he likes does not involve the obligation to insist that he is right.

The temper of the times is not congenial to the Christian claim for total allegiance. And the preacher must be as wise as a serpent and as gentle as a dove in his determined, persistent effort to clarify the issues, to win and to persuade, to attract and to convince. It does no good to alienate deliberately nor to antagonize intentionally. Yet to pussyfoot and beat around the bush is inexcusably reprehensible.

The need for firm and uncompromising espousal of a definite, articulate faith in the midst of the peculiarly confusing, superficial temper of our times has never been greater; to that end the preacher of today must devote his efforts and capacities with persistent zeal. He must not only set forth the firm, definite beliefs of the Christian Gospel but must also show his people the liberating power of living by a faith that is firm and definite. He must teach people what the Christian Religion *is* in an age which, for the most part, doesn't know, and then restore to popular consciousness the idea that to live by faith in Christ is an exciting adventure which gives new light and new joy to all life, and fulfills the highest capacities of every human soul.

10

Life and Death

THERE is more to this mystery of life than
meets the eye. This world, with all its fascinating and mysterious phenomena, is incidental to
purposes and meanings far greater and more en-
during, far more significant and complete than
anything discoverable within its own limited
bounds. This earthly creation and all the vast universes within universes, of which it is but a tiny
part, are perishable, transitory, and fragmentary.
They are a temporal part of an infinitely greater
whole. Above and beyond what we see and know
here is the quality of the eternal which we can perceive and experience only by faith. This life and
this world are a tale that is only partly told. Far
beyond our present ken there is a final purpose
and fulfillment of which this life and this observ-
able creation are truly a part—but only a part—
and which alone can make sense out of this part
which is otherwise no more than sound and fury,
chaos and illusion, mockery and torment.

All this is so basic to Christian teaching that it might seem, at first glance, to be too elementary to be mentioned. Nonetheless it is denied vigorously and stubbornly on every side—if not in theory at least in practice. And even for Christians, elementary though it be, it is the easiest thing in the world to forget or at least to be allowed to remain so far in the background of the conscious mind as to make inoperative its saving perspective. The immediacy of things and pleasures and responsibilities and worries makes fools of us all at the drop of a hat. "Thou fool! This night thy soul shall be required of thee" is a statement applicable not alone to the rich man in our Lord's parable; it is a statement applicable to all humanity in its preoccupation with the imperious demands of the world and the flesh.

One of the primary tasks of the Christian preacher is to keep constantly before his people the recollection of eternity and to remind them repeatedly of the necessity for choice and decision about the nature of this world in relation to eternity. Is this world the beginning and end of reality or is it but a part thereof? Every person must make up his own mind about this and proceed to live accordingly. And in either case it is an adventure of faith which is never free from the possibility of being wrong. As much as we might wish it were otherwise, life refuses us the easy way of demonstrable proof and demands of us a willful choice and decision.

This whole matter is brought into sharp focus by the problem of death. And that problem is one which keeps intruding upon the consciousness of even the most determined escapist. It is a problem from which no one can for very long be removed. If the likeliness of one's own death seems remote at any time, the death of his friends or relatives keeps bringing the whole subject back again immediately in front of his eyes. The problem of death continuously annoys and distresses and frightens or probes and stimulates and challenges mankind. It is a burr under the saddle of the materialist. It is a shadow which dogs the footsteps of the hedonist and haunts him with its leech-like persistence. To the superficial, it is a fearsome intruder which denies him peace save on its own terms. It makes everlastingly uneasy and restless the wary eye of the unrepentant sinner. It never ceases to mock and belittle the self-confidence of the "intellectual." Some people are paralyzed with fright at the approach of its presence or be-numbed with a kind of self-induced hypnosis when it touches life within the orbit of their immediate associations and relationships. Even the avowed skeptic who has chosen with firm purpose the road of the unbeliever finds that death retains the power to disturb. For if nothing else, he is forced to face with Hamlet the possibility of continued consciousness and self-awareness beyond the grave. "Perchance to dream! Aye, there's the rub."

For the Christian, death is a subject for sober reflection and for the testing of his faith, and it is a subject to which the preacher must refer frequently with the intent of helping people "make friends" with it. "In the midst of life we are in death," and until there is reconciliation with its inexorable presence, human life is lived under the load of a schizophrenic, artificial tension destructive of its intended quality.

Preach on the subject of death as part of God's beneficent scheme of things and as a potential experience of spiritual growth and progress for those who put their trust in Him. Point out that if it were not for death, only God knows the extent to which man would go in his spiritual self-destruction. Point out that death is one of God's controls whereby He curbs or sets limits to the dangerous gift of free-will which He has bestowed upon His creatures. It may even be that the fact of death has prevented the total atrophy of man's spiritual potential. It may be that the inescapable remindings of death constitute one of the chief blessings of a beneficent and loving God upon His wayward, headstrong children. In the setting of the Christian Faith, death may be regarded and proclaimed as evidence of God's love.

Death is to be preached as evidence of God's judgment as well as of His love. You must avoid as you would the plague any trace of the sentimental escapism of Mary Baker Eddy and all her ilk. You must skirt with firm and determined steps the moral vacuum of Universalism as a concept of automatic salvation. You must make clear the distinction between the pagan doctrine of immortality as found in Greek philosophy and the Christian doctrine of Resurrection. Death is never less than actual and real, never other than of solemn and profound significance. Death is never incidental for the individual and never divorced from God's judgment. Death does not cancel out all aspects of a man's moral life on this earth as though the eternal moral law were an illusion.

Hosts of people proceed on the assumption that

one can well run away from, and forget as far as the will allows, not only death but God Himself because "all will be well in the end no matter what."

It is extremely commonplace for people to beat around the bush and to pussyfoot whenever the subject of death arises. The phrase, "If anything happens to me" is carefully and persistently substituted for the good, forthright Anglo-Saxon words, "When I die"—All of which is a far cry indeed from the Christian attitude toward, and declaration of, the nature of death and the life of the world to come.

The subject of death must be a familiar part of the preaching of the Gospel. We must all be reminded of the shortness and uncertainty of human life. We must all be exhorted to "keep in our minds a lively remembrance of that great day in which we must give a strict account of our thoughts, words and actions to him, appointed the Judge of quick and dead." We must all be recalled to ask for "grace always to live in such a state that we may never be afraid to die." We must all be asked, "Are you ready and prepared to meet your God?" We must all make friends with death, which is so much a part of God's creation.

Christianity declares that Christ is Lord of life and death, that in His death and Resurrection He conquered death and that death has no dominion over Him nor over them that are His. "I am the resurrection and the life, saith the Lord; he that believeth on me, though he were dead, yet shall he live; and whosoever liveth and believeth in me, shall never die." Faith in the resurrection of the dead and the life of the world to come is a firm and definite aspect of the Christian Gospel and a tremendously significant part of it. All Christian preaching must be overshadowed and leavened by that aspect of the Faith, for it gives a new dimension to all human living and thinking.

The resurrection of the dead is an act of God, not an automatic reaction inherent in a so-called "life force." This creation is not a self-sustaining mechanism. Human beings have no inherent or undeniable right to imperishability. God is the Creator, we the creatures. He made us for His purpose and for His pleasure; He is bound by no rules or obligations other than of His own making. When He chooses, He denies death the power to destroy. We, God's creatures, are valuable only because He loves us. He does not love us because we are, to begin with, so intrinsically valuable in our own right. God raises above the power of death to destroy that which to Him is too precious to be destroyed—that is, precious because He so regards it.

The Christian belief in the resurrection of the dead is belief in the power and love and justice and goodness of God. And when we say we believe in "the resurrection of the body," we mean that we believe in the survival, by God's grace, of human individuality, or identity, as distinguished from a kind of impersonal, unidentified survival in a cosmic sea. It is *persons* who are valued and loved by God, not just the forces which animate them. Preachers must make clear what so easily confuses people in the use of the word "body" here. Although the dictionary indicates plainly the wide range of meanings in the word *body*, still it must be made explicit what is meant by this phrase of the Creed.

One of the numerous definitions of *body* in the dictionary is "the principal part of anything." That is as good a definition as another to indicate the true self of a man which inhabits or is clothed by the perishable flesh, and which God chooses to raise above the power of death to destroy. People ask why there is not some other word than *body* to be used in the Creed, since the same word also means the flesh. It is confusing, to be sure. But we can never simplify the real significance of all this; we are dealing with matters deeply mysterious by their very nature, and to change the words will never make them any simpler. Therefore, the age-old words continue to find a place in the Creed without alteration.

The Christian message in the presence of death is a triumphant and uncompromising one, with all the values of individuality and love and morality and justice and mercy conserved by the infinite will and power of God. Preach that message persistently and clearly. Against the background of it, lead your people to an honest and realistic attitude toward those dealings with death which are so very much a part of every clergyman's work. Much that is pagan and tawdry has come to be regarded as conventional at funerals. This must be dealt with gently and lovingly but nonetheless firmly, for people usually welcome guidance in these matters. A funeral is, in large part, the business of disposing of an earthly body. It is to be done with dignity and reverence because of what this earthly body represents. But we are not to attempt to run away from the fact that what we are disposing of is only the perishable earthly clothing of the "principal part," or person. *Never* refer to a body as "he" or "she," and emphatically remind your people not to do so. To refer in that way to a body is bound to stir up confusion. Do not encourage the centering of attention upon the body itself at the time of a funeral; the "principal part" is not the earthly body but the spirit.

To avoid overemphasis and over concentration of attention on the earthly body, the casket is closed by requirement of certain parishes at the time of the funeral service and not opened again. This proves very helpful in maintaining the right Christian perspective.

What is done to or with the physical body after death is not going to make the slightest difference in the status or condition of the person whose earthly clothing it was. To say of the funeral arrangements, "It is the last thing we can do for him and therefore, we must have everything as nice [i.e., as expensive] as possible," is utterly false. We have done the very last thing possible for him *before* he died except to pray for him. No pastor should ever permit to go unrebuked the idea that elaborate funeral arrangements constitute "doing something" for the departed.

Discourage the expenditure of large sums of money for expensive caskets, vaults, and monuments. Such things, together with "blankets" of flowers, artificial grass, the custom of "viewing the remains" (or "the reviewal," as it is ungrammatically called in the jargon of professional morticians), the common remark, "Doesn't he look natural?" (by which is meant, "Isn't it easy to imagine he is not really dead at all?")—all combine to produce an aura of unchristian character around our dealings with death. Such things confuse people and make harder the whole experience, despite their appearance as palliatives. Good, clear Christian preaching can do much to sharpen the right perspective in the face of so much which tends to blur and disturb it.

Christianity never denies the reality of sorrow and bereavement. It never denies the solemnity and import of death. It says, rather, that sorrow and bereavement can be transfigured and glorified so that they become springs from which flow light and strength. It says that just as death for the individual Christian is a door through which he is permitted to enter a new world, so it is a window for those left behind, through which they are permitted to see new spiritual vistas.

Death illuminates the spiritual inheritance of mankind as nothing else can. Even love has fallen short of death as a source of the most ennobling and perceptive insights of our literary heritage. And the Christian preacher finds the subject of death, and the teaching of the Gospel concerning it, a fruitful source of light and inspiration in his sermons.

Finally, avoid the obviously ridiculous attempt to describe in detail "the life everlasting." One can be very certain, if not of anything else under the sun, that when anyone begins to say what things are like beyond the grave he is talking through his hat, even if it be a cardinal's hat or a bishop's mitre. To describe details of purgatory as do the Romanists, or of hell fire as did the early Calvinists, or of the square-mileage of heaven as do the present-day professional evangelists, is all poppycock, not only because it is obviously imaginary and a kind of blasphemous affront to Him who has chosen to keep the curtain drawn, but also because it is so unnecessary and so uncalled for. You are not expected to fill the place of an authority on the conditions which prevail beyond the grave. And you will do well to desist from detailed or analytical speculation in the pulpit even though your approach be extraordinarily brilliant. This is an area where we are meant to proceed solely by faith. Trust and confidence in God's goodness and mercy are all that are available as mental and spiritual equipment for that journey, and for the Christian, that is enough. Man's vain curiosity and insistence upon knowing what is not meant to be known are to be crowded out with a new spirit of creatureliness and dependence and self-commitment. "Father, into thy hands I commend my spirit" is the prayer which a Christian hopes will rise spontaneously to his lips in the face of death.

And when it comes to a loved one, he should pray in this wise: "Father, into Thy hands I commend the spirit of my beloved. Forgive my grasping hold upon that which is Thine before mine. Forgive my rebellious reluctance to yield to Thee the one I want and need so much. Help Thou mine unbelief. Strengthen my infirmity. Fill my heart with trust. Fold my beloved 'closer to Thy mercy's breast.'"

How true it is that "in the midst of life we are in death." But the Christian Gospel never runs away from facts nor attempts to delude. On the contrary, it takes all the facts into consideration, no matter how hard or difficult or even fearsome they appear, and relates them to the power and love and mercy of God, until it is seen indeed that this is His world and that He is all in all.